PRAISE FOR *LOVE KINDNESS*

You can't hate a people and reach a people at the same time. So, in moments like this, when culture is changing and many Christians are angry, we need wise leaders to show a better way. That's exactly what Barry Corey does in *Love Kindness*. This will be an essential book for Christians as they engage the new cultural moment we are in.

ED STETZER
Executive director of LifeWay Research and senior fellow at the Billy Graham Center, Wheaton College

Barry Corey's reminder that Christians are called to "love kindness" is refreshing, convicting, and extremely timely. What if kindness became a more defining attribute of Christ-followers than defensiveness?

MARK BATTERSON
New York Times bestselling author of *The Circle Maker* and lead pastor of National Community Church

Deep disagreements often create strong frictions that at times flare up into hostilities and even wars. In this wise and compelling book Barry Corey draws on his personal and professional experience to offer an antidote: the forgotten virtue of kindness—not as a mere social lubricant of "niceness," but as a generous way of life modeled on Christ's. The proposal is simple but revolutionary: the world would change if people with deep disagreements agreed to be kind to one another. A very much needed book at this juncture of evangelical engagement with the broader culture.

MIROSLAV VOLF
Author of *Flourishing: Why We Need Religion in a Globalized World*, professor of theology at Yale Divinity School, and founding director of the Yale Center for Faith and Culture

Love Kindness is a sorely needed plea, written at what I believe is the most opportune time of my life. The changes in the culture are breathtaking: escalating racial tension and questions of gender identity, equality, and rights, along with much more, present us with a unique moment in history to be voices of grace and truth in the marketplace. Shouting or silence are not the paths to influence. Instead we need a third way, the way of kindness, expounded and exemplified by my friend Barry Corey.

BRYAN LORITTS
Pastor for Preaching and Mission of Trinity Grace Church, New York City

If ever there was a book that was desperately needed in our day, let me "kindly" say, it is *Love Kindness: Discover the Power of a Forgotten Christian Virtue*. What is required of Christian disciples is that we should "love kindness." Here is God's gift to a watching world where the shrill tone of yelling at each other keeps getting louder and more acrimonious by the hour. In this beautifully written volume, President Corey has gently urged Christians to respond not in kind, but with God's kindness and love. I warmly endorse Dr. Corey's book as one of the most important antidotes to a dangerous moment in our history.

WALTER C. KAISER JR.
President Emeritus of Gordon-Conwell Theological Seminary

Barry Corey is a kind man. He learned to be kind from his remarkable father. So Corey is well qualified—academically and spiritually— to write this book, a book that embodies the interesting approach of teaching different aspects of kindness through stories in his own life. For Corey, kindness is not niceness, adopting a position of compromise, or an expression of a desire to be received. Rather, it is having a firm center and soft edges, it is learning to be receivable, and it is learning to dialog with those with whom we disagree with kindness in the way of Jesus. The number of issues that divide us is multiplying each day. As a result, there never has been a time other than now when *Love Kindness* is so desperately needed. Get this book, read it, discuss it with your friends and those whom you oppose. You'll be glad you did.

J. P. MORELAND
Distinguished Professor of Philosophy at Biola University and author of *The Soul: How We Know It's Real and Why It Matters*

In a world of social media trolls and cable news shouting matches, people of goodwill everywhere are calling for a return to civility. Capable thinkers have addressed the issue philosophically and theologically. Barry Corey builds upon such foundational principles, but what makes this book distinctive is its narrative approach. Through real-world illustrations, Biola's president walks us through what kindness in action looks like on some of the most difficult issues of our day. Highly recommended.

GREGORY ALAN THORNBURY, PHD
President of The King's College

Barry Corey challenges believers in Jesus Christ to respond to the breathtaking cultural and moral changes around us with courage and kindness. *Love Kindness* is a road map for living in the world while not becoming part of it. Read it and take heart.

ROBERTA GREEN AHMANSON
Writer, philanthropist, and art patron

A warm, humane, funny but pungent book. Corey takes the reader into the real, day-to-day stuff of living and reflects on the practice of Christian kindness in the midst of all of this. He does so with poignant honesty and with real insight. Don't read this book if you don't want to be moved.

DAVID F. WELLS
Distinguished Research Professor at Gordon-Conwell Theological seminary

My friend Dr. Barry Corey has written an insightful and empowering book illustrating how kindness is a key that can unlock many closed doors. *Everyone* can and should strive to be kinder than we are. It's a fruit of the Spirit that requires deliberate effort to cultivate, but the results can be transformational.

JIM DALY
President of Focus on the Family

This book makes me realize we are in dire need of more people like my friend Barry Corey, people of startling authenticity and genuinely humble and joyful faith. But there's great news: if you read this book, you may well become such a person. You'll certainly begin that journey. I recommend it highly.

ERIC METAXAS
New York Times bestselling author of *Bonhoeffer* and host of the nationally syndicated *Eric Metaxas Show*

As compelling as it is convicting, *Love Kindness* shows how a life of selfless kindness can change the world for God's glory. This is Barry Corey at his finest. I highly recommend this for readers who want to better serve the kingdom of God.

D. MICHAEL LINDSAY
President of Gordon College

We evangelicals need this book. And the folks who see us as mean-spirited people need it too—to get a good picture of biblical fidelity at its best. Barry Corey makes the case for kindness with clarity and courage. In this book he has both inspired me and taught me!

RICHARD J. MOUW, PHD
President Emeritus and Professor of Faith and Public Life at Fuller
Theological Seminary

Niceness is quiet and passive, often to the demise of a person and of a culture. But kindness is courageous and truthful because of love. It will trade its own popularity to seek the highest good of others. In his life, in his face and voice, in his university, and in this good book, Barry Corey shows us the way of kindness. He leads.

KELLY MONROE KULLBERG
Author of *Finding God beyond Harvard: The Quest for Veritas*

Love Kindness is insightful, enjoyable, and inspiring. In an age when rancor and opposition seem to be ramping up, Dr. Corey challenges Christians to embrace the way of kindness. I found myself cheering at some points and personally convicted at others. As Christians, we are committed to biblical teaching. And yet, as *Love Kindness* so clearly portrays, we must live and teach that truth with genuine kindness towards others. My thanks to Dr. Corey for providing a helpful road map for how Christians can live both the grace and truth of Jesus in our world today.

SEAN MCDOWELL
Assistant professor of Christian Apologetics at Biola University, an
internationally acclaimed speaker, and the bestselling author of over fifteen
books, including *A New Kind of Apologist*

A thought-provoking, heart-stirring challenge to consider kindness as a barometer of a grace-shaped life.

ALISTAIR BEGG
Radio host and pastor on *Truth for Life*

Finally . . . please EVERY ONE of us who follow Christ, PLEASE read this book. Our starting point with people probably reveals much more about what's going on inside of us, and Barry points us to a kindness that shifts our soul and opens our heart. With a deft way with words, he captures the essence of a winsome civility that our world so desperately needs.

NANCY ORTBERG
Author of *Seeing in the Dark: Finding God's Light in the Most Unexpected Places*

Kindness is not niceness: a trivial virtue that is easy to fake. It is rather a radical commitment that calls every follower of Christ to costly love. We need more kindness in our homes, where—strangely—we are often at our worst with the people we love. We also need it in the church, where sometimes our behavior is even worse. And we need it most desperately of all in our personal relationships with people outside the Christian faith. Few leaders exemplify the kindness of Christ as consistently as Barry Corey, whose compelling stories and wise exhortations elevate this necessary virtue to its proper place in daily Christian life and the church's witness to the world.

DR. PHILIP G. RYKEN
President of Wheaton College

Barry Corey's radiant life and deeply personal, poignant, and often humorous book beautifully capture the kind of Christian I long to be: wise and winsome, courageous and civil, known for what I am *for* . . . not for what I am *against*. Live out the message of *Love Kindness* and you will find yourself less in a culture war and more like the early church, growing in favor with God and people.

KEN SHIGEMATSU
Pastor of Tenth Church Vancouver and bestselling author of *God in My Everything*

Having spent my career working in the media, I am convinced that one of the biggest reasons Christians are marginalized in our culture is the perception that we're bullies, trying to push our agenda on nonbelievers. That's why this could not be a better time for Dr. Barry Corey's new book, *Love Kindness*. This is more than a book. It's a strategy for transforming culture.

PHIL COOKE
Filmmaker, media consultant, and author of *Unique: Telling Your Story in the Age of Brands and Social Media*

Barry Corey lives in the tension every single day. His commitment to live with biblical conviction and never shy away from the most difficult questions makes him one of my go-to sources for wisdom and encouragement.

GABE LYONS
Q founder and author of *Good Faith*

With candor and winsomeness, Barry Corey confronts the way I think about my life. Kindness has always been attractive, but he makes it magnetic. With relentless precision and great stories, he shows again and again that kindness is found where grace and truth come together. His reach is broad—across the lines of race and ethnicity and theology and sexual orientation. So, when he calls the reader to aggressive kindness and "being receivable," it makes sense. At his father's memorial service in 1998, Barry asked me to read a letter he had written to his dad. I was honored beyond measure. That is precisely what I felt when I finished *Love Kindness*: honored. Read it. You'll see.

> **RICHARD FOTH**
> Coauthor with Mark Batterson of *A Trip around the Sun: Turning Your Everyday Life into the Adventure of a Lifetime*

Love Kindness is a much-needed reframing of the cultural conversations of our day. *How* Christians express their allegiance to Jesus in the world is just as important as *that* they do so. Dr. Barry Corey invites us to again consider the way of Jesus and the postures of heart he embodied in his ministry. This book is a clear, compelling call to reexamine how Christians engage the culture. Highly recommended.

> **MIKE ERRE**
> Pastor, author, and teacher

While many books address faith and culture, I've yet to find one like *Love Kindness*. As I turned each page, I continually found myself convicted and challenged. Kindness is an uncompromising trait that all Christians should possess. We can all thank Barry Corey for writing this book and pushing us further toward what it means to follow Jesus.

> **CALEB KALTENBACH**
> Lead pastor of Discovery Church

Barry Corey has written an important book, which I thoroughly enjoyed. He advocates true kindness without reducing it to mere cosmetic niceness. Too many Christians choose between standing for truth and demonstrating grace, and the result is self-righteous meanness disguised as truth or indifferent tolerance disguised as grace. *Love Kindness* attempts to avoid both errors, and it's full of both grace and truth, with warm and heart-touching stories. (I was particularly moved by the example of Barry's dad.) The church today desperately needs the humility that rejects mean-spirited religion and exemplifies kindness while upholding biblical truth. You needn't agree with everything in this book to profit from it immensely—it will make you think, reflect, and see yourself as others may see you. Most important, it may prompt you to ask Jesus, "Will you help me to love kindness?"

> **RANDY ALCORN**
> Author of *The Grace and Truth Paradox* and *Happiness*

Discover the Power of
a Forgotten Christian Virtue

love
KINDNESS

BARRY H. COREY

Tyndale House Publishers, Inc.
Carol Stream, Illinois

Library of Congress Cataloging-in-Publication Data

Corey, Barry H.
   Love kindness : discover the power of a forgotten Christian virtue / Barry H. Corey.
      pages cm
   Includes bibliographical references.
   ISBN 978-1-4964-1157-0 (hc) — ISBN 978-1-4964-1196-9 (sc)   1. Kindness—Religious aspects—Christianity.   I. Title.
   BV4647.K5C67 2016
   241'.4—dc23   2015033840

Printed in the United States of America

22   21   20   19   18   17   16
 8   7   6   5   4   3   2

CONTENTS

INTRODUCTION

As God's chosen people, holy and dearly loved,
clothe yourselves with . . . kindness.
—COLOSSIANS 3:12

I held the hand of the kindest man I ever knew, sitting by his bedside in silent reverence while he lay shrouded in sheets bleached white.

We were alone in a Boston palliative care room, just the two of us except for a hospice nurse occasionally interrupting the holy to adjust a drip or check a vital. Room 402 was sacred space.

I looked at him that night as he looked at nothing, and I shook my head at the cruelty of cancer. After three years of potent drugs, radiation, wheelchairs, epidurals, and horrible pain that drove him to weeping, he never asked, "Why me?" When visitors walked into his room, even during his last days, he made *them* the honored guests. I thought about his kindness that night as the sounds of his irregular breathing softened.

By morning, my father—the kindhearted reverend—was dead.

Years later, what I recall is not his courage in death. It is his kindness in life. His kindness was the open door for friends and strangers to enter.

I had never given serious thought to the revolutionary power of kindness until my father died. Then I started paying attention to the stories told about him. He wasn't quickly forgotten. His gentle influence rippled on and continues to ripple on. The stories were neither about his commanding leadership nor about his well-known status. He didn't start a company, earn much money, make the news, hold public office, or write a book. No one would have drafted his Wikipedia page.

The stories were about his spirit of kindness. His influence ran deep and wide, showing up in kindness lavished liberally. He was wildly welcoming, epic in life because he was epic in love.

I'm just now beginning to grasp how uncommon kindness is. My father's example doesn't seem to characterize the tone of conversations many Christians are having today in the public square. Kindness has become far too often a forgotten virtue. Christians often bypass kindness to begin a shouting match, or we just talk among ourselves about how awful the other side is. We have ranted before we've related, deeming the latter too soft on sin. Christians—and I've seen this especially in American Christians in recent years—have employed the combative strategy, and it's not working. The "culture wars" have done little to change our society, and we've lost many if not all of these wars. As a result, the church too often is marginalized and mocked, and increasingly people are viewing the Bible as just as intolerable as our aggressive tactics.

To be Christian, kindness must shape us and define us. But this powerful virtue seems to be characterizing us less and not more. We have lost an understanding of the power of kindness, mistakenly dismissing it as fluff or flat. Kindness needs to be rediscovered.

Our reflex is to fight those who oppose us. Standing for our dignity and in defense of the truths we hold, we have too often led with harshness toward those antagonistic to the Christian faith. To prove we're not going soft on our faith (and sometimes understanding that fighting words raise more money), we're quick to label others from a distance. Leaders have been known to whip their supporters into a frenzy over the antics of their political, media, or theological "enemies."

I wrote this book out of frustration that those who represent the gospel are often caustic and harsh, picking fights with those whose views are hostile to theirs. In other words, Christians are often starting with *unkindness*. Unkindness has little effect beyond marshaling other Christians to admire our toughness and raising our own profile. This has gotten us nowhere in the cause of the gospel, our Christian call to be redemptive voices to that which is broken.

Our increasingly shrill sounds in the public square are not strengthening our witness but weakening it. Bullhorns and fist shaking—mustering armies and using war-waging rhetoric—are far less effective than the way of kindness, treating those with whom we disagree with charity and civility.

That doesn't mean we don't stand courageously for what we deem right, true, and just. But kindness is not incompatible with courage. Kindness embodies courage, although courage does not always embody kindness. Too often our centers are firm on conviction, but our edges are also hard in our tactics. This way is characterized by aggression.

And on the other hand there is the way of "niceness." Whereas aggression has a firm center and hard edges, niceness has soft edges and a spongy center. Niceness may be pleasant, but it lacks conviction. It has no soul. Niceness trims its sails to prevailing cultural winds and wanders aimlessly, standing for nothing and thereby falling for everything.

Kindness is certainly not aggression, but it's also not niceness. Niceness is cosmetic. It's bland. Niceness is keeping an employee in the job, knowing he's no longer the right fit but failing him *and* the company because you don't have the courage to do the kind thing. Kindness calls you to tell him he's not the person for the position and then dignify him in the transition.

Kindness is fierce, never to be mistaken for niceness. They're not the same and never were. Kindness is neither timid nor frail, as niceness can be so easily. *Kindness* is all over the Bible, plentiful in both Testaments. But you won't find *niceness* there once—or *nice*, for that matter. The ideals of kindness are rooted in Scripture, founded on Christian theology, and tested over the millennia by followers of Jesus. Since the early church, disciples have walked the risky and sometimes dangerous road of kindness.

In today's polarized culture, we are often pulled toward one extreme or the other, soft centers or hard edges. I'm proposing a different approach, a third way. Rather than the harshness of firm centers and hard edges, and rather than the weakness of spongy centers and soft edges, why don't we start with kindness? Kindness is the way of firm centers and soft edges.

This book is an attempt to explain what this means—not so much to define as to describe it as I've seen it in different people from different settings. My hope is that the stories I tell will help you understand what a firm center and soft edges looks like in your life.

It's time for followers of Jesus to rediscover the power of kindness. Kindness is a biblical way of living. It's a fruit of the Holy Spirit on Paul's short list in Galatians 5. It's not a duty or an act. It's the natural result of the Holy Spirit's presence in our lives. We exhale kindness after we inhale what's been breathed into us by the Spirit. Kindness radiates when we're earnest about living the way of Christ, the way of the Spirit. Kindness displays the wonder of Christ's love through us.

Many Christians nowadays tend to talk with bravado and bluster about heroism that impacts the world. I'd rather talk about the power of kindness to change lives, ours and others'. Paul got this when he said to Jesus' followers in Rome that God's kindness leads us to repentance (see Romans 2:4). Repentance, more than anything else, changes lives. And kindness leads us there.

Kindness is not a virtue limited to grandmothers or Boy

Scouts. We devalue its power when we think of kindness as pampering or random acts. Kindness doesn't pamper, and it's not random. It's radical. It is brave and daring, fearless and courageous, and at times, kindness is dangerous. It has more power to change people than we can imagine. It can break down seemingly impenetrable walls. It can reconcile relationships long thought irreparable. It can empower leaders and break stalemates. It can reconcile nations. Kindness as Jesus lived it is at the heart of peacemaking and has the muscle to move mountains. It's authentic and not self-serving.

Don't sell kindness short.

Kindness enables us to negotiate in a time when negotiating is dying and friendly discussions are yielding to rancor. Kindness—the higher ground—helps us find middle ground *and* common ground.

The greatest leadership influence lies ahead for those who walk the way of kindness in an increasingly fragmented and skeptical society. It's a path that will help us to be stronger leaders, more winsome neighbors, healthier husbands, better mothers, truer friends, more effective bosses, and faithful disciples.

Kindness is strong yet humble. Kindness is honesty and looks like truth with love. The psalmist David believed this, writing, "Let a righteous man strike me—that is a kindness; let him rebuke me—that is oil on my head" (Psalm 141:5).

This is our challenge: living from a Christ-centered core that spills out into a life of kindness. It's a life with a firm center and soft edges.

For many of us, venturing into the way of kindness will be hard. It's countercultural. It's risky. It's sometimes unwelcome and awkward. It's admitting our own messiness and imperfections on the journey.

This book's title, *Love Kindness*, comes from Micah, the Old Testament prophet who asks on behalf of Israel, "With what shall I come before the LORD?" (Micah 6:6). Micah answers his question with a few hollow suggestions that are in fact external religious rites, each of increasing value. Burnt offerings of calves? One thousand rams? Ten thousand rivers of oil? Our firstborn sons?

None of these is sufficient. Rather, the Lord's reply of what he requires is a simple threefold response of obedience: "To do justice, and to love kindness, and to walk humbly with your God" (Micah 6:8, ESV). *Love* kindness. We don't "just do" kindness in some Nike-esque way. We are to *love* kindness. Perhaps the Scriptures so often use the term *loving-kindness* to make sure we don't separate *love* from *kindness*.

"Love kindness" is the partner of "do justice." If doing justice is the firm center, then loving kindness is the soft edges. Both are what God expects of us, not one or the other. And we do both of these with equal passion while walking humbly with God.

Love kindness. We need this more than ever. It's time for us to love kindness and in so doing rediscover the revolutionary force of this fading Christian virtue.

"To love kindness" seems like it should be an easy task for us—who *doesn't* love kindness? Kindness is easy to show to the coffee barista when she gets our latte right. Kindness comes naturally to our family so long as there's harmony. But kindness is much harder to show those we might have previously ignored, avoided, judged, or condemned. Kindness is a tougher road when we live in tension with colleagues or in our marriage. Try walking the way of kindness then. Kindness is not intuitive. But Jesus calls us to demonstrate the power of kindness to everyone we come across. Neighbor or stranger. Wife or son. Colleague or enemy.

More profoundly, kindness calls us to the risk of encountering people with disease, those living outside of grace, and even those who would threaten to harm or destroy us. What does kindness look like when we extend it to our enemies or the outcast, the bullied or the lonely, the unsavory or the unlovely? What does it look like to be kind to the persecutors of Christians and not just the persecuted?

Jesus nevertheless calls us to the way of kindness—selfless, humble, vulnerable, open, risky, and faithful. He has called us to extraordinary kindness. Kindness opens us to adventurous relationships and the joyful journey we otherwise would miss.

The good news is that kindness has the potential to be contagious. When otherwise inconsequential, indifferent, marginalized, proud, stubborn, condemned individuals receive our genuine kindness, true connection with God can begin. And often they who have received our kindness then pay it forward.

The way of kindness is the answer for how Christians need to position themselves, especially today. Kindness is risky, revolutionary, unconventional, costly, and hard. These are also the adjectives that define what it truly means to follow Jesus.

I wrote this book as an alternative to the voices of barbed-wire-wrapped Christians who are picking fights from pulpits, blogs, talk shows, town meetings, or political platforms. I also wrote this book to demonstrate that kindness is not anemic or convictionless. Rather, it has the power to influence others, revealing the truth and grace of the Christian faith far more than the insecurity of confrontational posturing.

I wrote this book for me, the ordinary guy who grew up wanting to live a life of meaning without meanness. I wrote this book for people like me who have discovered kindness as the antidote to struggles with fear and insecurity: the fear that we've fooled people into thinking we're special and the insecurity that rears its head in our own pride. I wrote this book to recover in my own life the revolutionary way Jesus called us to live. The way of selfless risks. The way of staggering hope. The way of authenticity. The way of profound love. The way of becoming the "kind" kind. I've got a long way to go, but I want to grasp the power of kindness the way Jesus intended it to be lived.

I wrote this book because as a university president, I care about how the rising generation lives out the way of Jesus in an increasingly polarized and mean-spirited culture. So I'm posing the idea of living the way of kindness, a way that is mercy filled, reverent, and God fearing. Kindness is a dimension of God's common grace through us. It's a civility grounded in gentleness and respect. At the same time, kindness is neither milquetoast nor weak. It is fierce and passionate. The God-authored spirit of kindness in us has the power to upend the enemy and season the world around us for the good. Kindness as Jesus lived it presents the highest hope for a renewal of Christian civility, a renewal needed now more than ever.

As my friend Bryan Loritts wrote me when I told him I was embarking on this book, "We've tried legalism, and that has proven inept and unattractive. Some are trying a warped form of love that renders us saltless. The only thing that works is a life that embodies grace and truth lived out in relationship with others." I call that kindness—a life with a firm center and soft edges.

My prayer is that this book gives rise to a call to live and love the forgotten way of kindness. A life that calls us to risk. A life that calls us to hope. A life that calls us to love. And the life Christ invites us to follow.

Chapter 1

A FATHER'S PROFOUND LESSON: THE WAY OF KINDNESS CALLS US TO BE RECEIVABLE

Whoever receives you receives me, and whoever

receives me receives him who sent me.

—MATTHEW 10:40, ESV

For my father's final days, we checked him into a Boston hospice center, referring to it as "palliative care" to mask the gravity of his last home. It was a welcoming room housing a welcoming man, and visitors sensed in this antiseptic environment the purity of my father's affections. As long as he was cogent, he was also kind.

Loving-kindness was my father's greatest way to help others see their greatest yearning: knowing the grace of God the Father. For him, it always began by making himself what he called "receivable." When he went into the receivable mode, he would reach out to others with love that could only be described as divine. That life of being receivable is the starting point for the life of kindness. And as his life flashed before my eyes on that last night, I recalled one of the most profound lessons he ever taught me.

My father lived the receivable life, but he talked to me about it only once. One somewhat ordinary conversation on an early morning walk with him in Bangladesh stands out as that transformative moment when I began to grasp how his acts of being receivable were the first steps toward kindness.

I was researching in Bangladesh for several months when my father visited for a few days, traveling with my mother between missionary stops in Madras and Singapore. I was in my late twenties, ponytailed and single. Each morning before breakfast, he and I descended the staircase from the small flat I leased and stepped onto the streets of Dhaka, one of the world's poorest and most densely populated cities. On our walk we passed half-constructed homes framed by bamboo scaffolding. Dumpsters were permanent, not portable, made of brick and rummaged through simultaneously by dogs and children and widows. Open drains on each side of the street reeked of human waste, and rickshaw peddlers dodged us as we walked our morning route.

For the three or four days we were together, we spent much of our time catching up on all that was happening in each other's lives. He was particularly interested in what I was seeing and observing. This was nothing new.

But one morning our walk seemed different—quieter and more contemplative. As we turned the first corner, he shared with me that five decades after he began his pilgrimage of faith, there was so much about God's wisdom and ways that he still did not know. He held no seminary degree. He never completed college. But as we walked, Hugh Corey—the follower of God—began to share with me what his life in Christ had taught him.

"And he that taketh not his cross, and followeth after me," he spoke in his native King James language, recounting the words of Christ near the end of Matthew 10, "is not worthy of me. He that findeth his life shall lose it: and he that loseth his life for my sake shall find it." Finally, he camped on the next sentence, the point of his recitation: "He that receiveth you receiveth me, and he that receiveth me receiveth him that sent me."

Then he stopped talking for a few minutes, and I considered the last part of Christ's words my father had just recited: "Whoever receives you receives me, and whoever receives me receives him who sent me."

I'm not sure my father grasped the full context of what Jesus was saying in that verse, but I'm certain he did understand what Jesus modeled in the Gospels: a receivable life. Love your enemies. Receive a child in Jesus' name. Pray for those who persecute you. When you're slapped on the cheek, turn the other. Listen to the shunned harlot. Talk to the scorned tax collector. When someone takes your coat, give him your shirt. When someone tells you she wants you to walk a mile with her, walk two.

Whoever receives you receives me. These are the instructions

...us gave one day to his disciples, prescribing for them what it means to be a faithful follower.

Knowing I was the student that moment as we turned onto the next street, I waited for my father to continue. He told me that in everything he did, he would choose to make himself receivable to the people God placed in his life.

He actually used the word *receivable*. This was the word that made him tick. I don't know if I've heard other followers of Jesus refer to themselves that way, but the word works for me. My father gave me the vocabulary to articulate his way of life and to help me understand it in mine.

He stopped walking and turned to me. "Barry," he said, "if the lives God intersects with mine don't have the opportunity to receive me, how will they ever know the love God has for them?" I nodded.

What he was saying made sense in light of everything I'd seen him say and do in all our years together. He started walking again, and I fell in beside him.

"I've got to live my life so strangers, friends, aching, lonely, family—they receive me," he said. "And through me they see God's inexhaustible love."

We finished our walk in silence. I knew that although he wanted to share with me his musings as he had so many times before and would do so many times after, this moral was different. It was as if he had traveled halfway around the world just to find me and bequeath a truth. Maybe it was different because I had not heard his voice for many months. Maybe it was different because I was trying to make sense of my life in Christ while I lived among crowds of the world's poorest. Maybe it was different because I was ready to hear what he had to say. Maybe the Holy Spirit was speaking to me through a holy mouthpiece. I don't know.

This I do know: I have gone back to that walk many times. And as I have, I know that God ordained *that* moment when I would receive a cherished gift. On the fetid streets of Bangladesh—as from the local mosque the muezzin was calling Muslims to prayer—the bedrock of Hugh Corey's Christian faith was passed on to me, my father's son.

Two days after he spoke, I witnessed his demonstration of the profound power of the receivable life.

Shamsul was a poor Bangladeshi man of twenty-one who rented a bed in the servants' quarters behind the house where I lived. He spoke little English and, like many others, left his family in their village to seek work as a day laborer in Dhaka, Bangladesh's largest city.

I noticed my father begin to build a relationship with Shamsul in the few days since he arrived, something I honestly had not done. For my father, this was nothing new. All my life I saw him show love to schoolteachers, wayfarers, disgraced pastors, dentists, tailors, attorneys, and on and on. But it was not until after our walk earlier in the week that I had pondered how his life imitated the transforming power of Christ's words: "Whoever receives you receives me, and whoever receives me receives him who sent me."

Then it happened. The receivable moment occurred between Hugh Corey and Shamsul when the words of Christ, as they had so often before, called my father to show his radical kindness.

I was transfixed as this sixty-eight-year-old Canadian preacher reached out his hands in a moment of outpouring compassion and—as I had witnessed many times before—held another person's face in his grip. I was willing to bet on what was coming next, and I would have won.

"Shamsul, my friend," the Canadian preacher said, "I love you." Then pulling my father's face to his, Shamsul leaned forward and kissed him right on the head. On one day in Bangladesh my father told me what kindness looked like. A few days later he showed me.

Over the years I've been quick to relegate the way of kindness to someone who is simpler, who is less of a leader than I am. I'm quick to conclude that some people have the knack for kindness, but it's not my thing. I'm too busy, too proud, too shy, too apathetic, too fearful, too macho, too passive, too oblivious. When I do this, I'm missing the point that for followers of Jesus, it's not an option but a mandate, not an occasion but a lifestyle. This has been my struggle for the better part of my life.

We're okay with occasional acts of kindness, but a *life* of kindness? That's for those less burdened by the strains of responsibility and who have a lot more margin to pencil kindness moments into their schedules. Kindness is too soft for leaders.

But the Bible never talks about kindness as a gift you either have or you don't. It describes kindness as a fruit of the Spirit, a virtue that is meant to grow from all Christians, even when other people don't like the kindness they see in us.

This may sound counterintuitive, but the objective of the receivable life is not to be received, but to be receiv*able*. The goal of the kind life is not to be thanked; it is to be obedient. Whether or not the grocery clerk or the college professor receives my overtures of kindness should not be my concern. Jesus never said we would be received. He simply said we need to make ourselves receivable—that is, to remove the distance or the obstacles that keep others from seeing Jesus within us. In fact, Jesus said that sometimes, despite our lives of grace, we will *not* be received. We can expect, then, to be ignored, rejected, or even persecuted. He even assures us of solidarity with him when we are snubbed, affirming in the Gospel of Luke that "whoever rejects you rejects me; but whoever rejects me rejects him who sent me" (10:16).

I sometimes confuse living to be received and living to be receivable. Living to be received focuses on how others respond to my kindness. This is out of my control. Not only that, but living to be received ultimately inflates my ego. Living to be receivable is different. It decreases the ego because it's kindness that is not awaiting a thank-you. Living the way of kindness should not be measured by how people perceive me. Living the way of kindness calls us to a posture of humility, and humility is most authentically lived when I accept that my kindness will sometimes be rejected. Kindness focuses on how I open myself for others to receive me, whether they choose to or not.

Those who live the receivable life make it easy for some to love them. They also make it easy for some to despise them. But they don't make it easy for anyone to forget them. Kindness always stands out.

The alchemy we need as Christians to impact the world for the cause of Christ is to make ourselves receivable, to live the way of radical kindness. Even our enemies will know we are Christians by our love, though we may continue in the crosshairs of their scorn. To many around the world, Christ's love *for* us and *through* us is offensive.

Sometimes Christians raise eyebrows in our own faith communities when we engage in conversation with people or groups who believe far differently than we do. My father himself certainly raised a few eyebrows. It's easier—and sometimes more fun—to cast stones from the outside than to engage winsomely through building friendships, what Jesus models as the way of kindness.

I hear myself telling university students that they need to live in this humble posture of being receivable, of being kind. Of course we need to stand up and fight for convictions that are under attack, but more often combative and defensive posturing ought to give way to listening and civility, even with those we see as ideological opponents. Kindness means being more concerned with what we are for than what we are against. Kindness means taking off the steel-toed boots used to kick Jesus into our culture or to kick heresies out of our brothers and instead walking barefoot, the very position Jesus' disciples took when he washed their feet and told them to do likewise. We need a firm center and soft edges. We need to tone down the saber rattling, the fist shaking, the scowled conversations, the voice raising.

The way of kindness is not just having right theology; it's being the right kind of people. It's understanding that our lives as Jesus' followers mean we have a common humanity with everyone, and therefore there's no need for exceptionalism. We owe all human beings the honor due them as beings made in the image of God.

Being receivable is Rick Warren saying yes to an invitation to address a gathering of Muslims, or Chuck Colson reaching across the aisle with Catholics, or Focus on the Family's Jim Daly initiating a quiet conversation with pro-choice activists to promote foster care. Being receivable happens when pastors stand up against the bullying and the harsh discrimination against those in their communities who identify as LGBT. To many in the church, this kind of kindness is awkward and risky. It makes some of us uneasy. It sometimes backfires. But erring on the side of being too kind is far better than never trying to build a bridge at all. The isolationism and overconfidence often characteristic of Christian fundamentalism can be relaxed without relaxing the gospel on which we stand.

My father took a risk that erring on the side of kindness was worth it. I still find myself stopping to think about what Jesus meant when he said, "Whoever receives you receives me" and then went on to say, "Whoever receives me receives him who sent me." By extension, when we make ourselves receivable in

Jesus' name, representing him, those who receive us receive Jesus and the Father as well. This doesn't mean that by receiving us, they receive forgiveness for their sins. But it does mean that by receiving us, they get a taste of what it's like to know God's boundless and unconditional love.

The receivable life is the risky way, the Jesus way, the way of kindness. It becomes a habit of the heart, a fruit of the Spirit that is abundant and ripe. We are called to make a difference in the world for the good, and we will not go far making a difference without embracing and being embraced by the power of kindness.

Chapter 2

A NEW JOB, A ROAD TRIP, A FATHER AND SON:
THE WAY OF KINDNESS IS MESSY

*By faith Abraham, when called to go to a place he
would later receive as his inheritance, obeyed and went,
even though he did not know where he was going.*

—HEBREWS 11:8

After a lifetime in New England, our family would make the big move. I'd been offered the presidency of a Christian university in Southern California. My wife, our three kids, and I would uproot from the certain and head three thousand miles toward uncertainty.

To ease the transition and maybe chronicle a family adventure or two, I envisioned a road trip, the whole family watching the cultural and scenic frames of America change as East became Middle became West. Sing-alongs with dad in the driver's seat. Breakfasts at Cracker Barrel playing frivolous rounds of the triangle-peg game while awaiting our Sunrise Samplers. We'd pose for family photos outside

DC's Jefferson Memorial, Nashville's Grand Ole Opry, Memphis's Lorraine Motel, the Alamo in San Antonio. On the highways, I'd play recordings of Garrison Keillor's *A Prairie Home Companion* as the mile markers passed. The children would recollect favorite family moments, Paula would read passages from Scripture, and we'd pass our time with long stretches of silence. It was the perfect trip—in my imagination.

In the middle of contacting real estate agents and moving companies, deciding what to keep and what to give away, I unveiled to the family my blissful plans of how we'd get to California. My wide eyes and hand gestures were greeted by long stares and limp arms. Paula spoke first, quickly pointing out a logistical problem.

"Barry, we just gave our minivan to missionaries," rendering our Volvo sedan a tight squeeze for five, not to mention Holly, our dog. "Sorry. I'm out."

Ella, eleven, immediately seconded. Sam, eight and finishing grade two, liked the idea until I told him we'd be in the car for eight days. So far, I was oh for three.

In Anders, our fourteen-year-old, I saw a crack.

"I don't know, Dad," he said, but I sensed something short of resolve in his voice.

"C'mon. Just the two of us, cross-country, father-son journey of a lifetime?"

"It's really far."

"I know," I told him, "but you'll see America and check more states off your list." We keep lists.

Studying his fingernails and shuffling his feet, he muttered, "Not sure I'm interested."

I still had an ace to play. One word might get him to fold.
"Baseball."

"Huh?"

"Just you and me, visiting baseball parks, major and minor, from coast to coast. America's sport. Your passion."

The corners of his mouth began to tilt up, a breakthrough in the negotiations. Anders's zeal for baseball had begun in elementary school. He memorized statistics and sought pregame autographs behind the Red Sox dugout. He replayed great moments over and over in his mind and recalled with precise detail the most obscure plays. Anders was Red Sox Nation packaged in a boy's body, and his passion had continued to the present day.

"Okay, Dad," he agreed. "If baseball's part of the deal, I'm in. We'll go together to California." Finally, I had a recruit to join me on the big road trip, the thrilling ride.

This should have been exciting, but if you had scratched the surface of my emotions, it would have been evident that this was a trip I dreaded. We weren't just heading to the state of California. We were heading to the state of uncertainty. In all of the excitement about the big road trip to the big job, my hands sweated and my throat lumped. I was playing the cool and collected one, but it was a lie.

Too often followers of Jesus are misled into believing our image will suffer when we remove the "we have our act together" front. But often the way of kindness means we admit we don't have it all together, that our lives are untidy and imperfect.

Authenticity is kindness because it allows others to see our struggles rather than hiding them behind feigned perfection. Authenticity is kindness when it admits our imperfections and uncertainties, our fears and anxieties.

Kindness involves the willingness to come out from behind my projected invincibility and acknowledge that my life is messy and uncertain. As counterintuitive as it might seem, when others see our authenticity, we become more attractive and more approachable. We become more *receivable.* This is a powerful dimension of living the way of kindness, owning up to the truth that we don't always know where we're going. Vulnerability, far more than name-dropping, endears us to others in a deep way. Yet we often hide behind our safe personas—Latin for the masks actors wore in ancient theater—rather than unmasking ourselves in the face of uncertainty.

For many of us, anxieties reside in the depths of our souls. Our marriages struggle, our kids wander, our friendships come and go, our careers stall, and our money evaporates. We fight depression and can't control our weight. Our prayer life is in Death Valley, and we've agreed to lead the church's class on prayer. We read the Christmas cards from families blowing their own horns, and we feel lacking. All the while we think we're not supposed to admit our flaws and fears.

I've been the poster child for this kind of thinking too many times.

Now that the new job was official, during those house-packing weeks I found myself vacillating between fist pumping and wiping anxiety's perspiration from my brow. I told others how stoked I was to take on the challenge of the presidency. I told myself, especially in the middle of the night, I was scared. That's usually when fear rears its hideous head. The imminent move exposed the truth that the uncertainties accompanying this major change frightened me. Though I didn't talk about my fears, except to Paula, I've learned in the years since accepting the job that something disarming happens when I let the guard down and let more folks in. This is a powerful gesture of loving-kindness.

Some people in my life are close enough that I tell them more of my messiness. But no one I meet should ever sense that my life is without anxieties and challenges. Kindness calls us to genuineness.

And the truth is life is always a journey into uncertainty. A job is terminated. A promotion is offered. A spot appears. A question is popped. A son comes out. A daughter checks out. An aging parent forgets. A deal falls apart. A friend bolts. Colleagues betray. A moving truck comes. Romance blows up in your face. A pregnancy test returns positive. Or negative . . . again.

I felt uncertainty raw and real when I was offered the Biola University presidency—a mixture of stomach-churning angst and trusting God that obedience is worth it. I felt like the dad who brought his tormented son to Jesus and flayed his soul, saying, "Lord, I believe. Help me in my unbelief" (see

Mark 9:24). I don't buy the idea that abiding serenity should accompany every risky thing we do, otherwise Mark wouldn't have recalled that "help me in my unbelief" line in his Gospel. But I do believe that peace will show up on the other side of the risky venture, sooner or later.

So we as a family of five obeyed and went, even though we did not know how the next chapter of our life would pan out.

Abraham obeyed and went, even though he did not know where he was going.

Sixty percent of the family made it clear to me that the cross-country family road trip wasn't happening. But I took consolation in hooking my eldest with the baseball stadium bait—the best bribe I could offer. I began to see the long drive as a way to deepen my bond with Anders, our firstborn, then fourteen, as baseball had always been an important part of our relationship. The truth was, I also needed an eight-day drive to grapple with my haunting anxieties of uprooting from the familiar for the uncertain.

I set out the terms for the trip. Anders could pick the route across America based on home games. We needed to be able to drive to the next ballpark neither with too much time wasted nor at a police-provoking speed. He'd do the ballpark research, come up with the road map, and buy the tickets online. I gave him my credit card and a price range, a potential hazard in retrospect. If he found the string of home games across the top of the country—cities like Pittsburgh, Toledo, Chicago, Minneapolis, and Seattle—we'd drive the high-numbered interstates. If the games were through the middle of the country—Allentown, St. Louis, Kansas City, and Denver—then off we'd plow into the Heartland.

Baseball had become our love language over the years.

I framed Anders's first bat, a once-blue, tired, and chipped cut of ash, his first wooden piece of slugging lumber. Its notches and scars remind me of the countless hours he swung this bat in our front yard, taking cuts at my reckless and random pitches. And when no baseballs were there to hit, he'd swing at stones or anything nonliving that could be thrown. Sometimes I'd watch him on our cul-de-sac with his bat just whiffing at the air.

I also framed his first Red Sox cap, worn thin. Its frayed bill told the story of a boy gripped by his hometown team. The old-fashioned and iconic *B* was embroidered front and center. Those were priceless days when I came home from work and, whenever the spirit moved me—and it often did—asked him if he wanted to head to Boston for a Sox game, which I often had access to as a member of the clergy. He'd check the *Boston Globe* or our Red Sox refrigerator magnet schedule to see who was in town, though I knew it didn't matter. He'd say yes whether we were playing the loathed Yankees or the pitiful Royals, in cold weather or looming thunderstorms, day or night. He never said no.

A Fenway Frank halfway through the game and a rousing rendition of "Sweet Caroline" made the game complete, win or lose, but especially if it was a win. Every time, my joy came from watching him watch baseball.

The Red Sox teased Anders, me, and Boston season after

season before inevitably breaking our yielding hearts. Season 2003 concluded with deep grief after Yankee Aaron Boone's game-seven homer off the Red Sox knuckler Tim Wakefield. It was David Halberstam who caught this quote while interviewing a die-hard Sox fan: "The path to understanding Calvinism in modern America . . . begins at Fenway Park." We were predestined to collapse.

But the saints persevered. Season 2004 concluded with glory and not groans. After that American League game seven come-from-behind division-series-of-the-ages against A-Rod and the Yankees, an oasis appeared in the World Series desert. We prayed it wasn't another mirage.

Paula and I woke our three children late that night for the final innings of game four against the St. Louis Cardinals. We wouldn't let them miss history, eighty-four years eluded. We watched together that immortal play as Edgar Rentería grounded to pitcher Keith Foulke, who trotted toward first, tossing the ball to a waiting Doug Mientkiewicz. The curse reversed, the Coreys along with all of Red Sox Nation proclaimed, "Finally!"

For me, Red Sox games with my firstborn were a few of my favorite things. Entering a ballpark on tickets bought or tickets given, standing hatless for the national anthem, and hearing the words "Play ball!"

But now we were leaving Boston once and perhaps for all to embark on "the drive." As Anders and I headed out of town for our move to California, I felt the loss not just of our town but of my boy, now becoming a man.

Fourteen, and his fleeting years of childhood entered the final innings.

"We're going south, Dad," Anders told me after he mapped the optimal route for our cross-country baseball tour. The best route he'd found started in Boston and then went to DC, dropping down to Charlotte and Atlanta, crossing westward through Amarillo to Albuquerque and ending in Anaheim, where we'd see the Red Sox twice play the Angels. Five major league games and two minor league games.

My agreement with Anders was to live baseball with him from coast to coast. But I told him about another part of the deal. We were going to eat our way across the country without once stepping foot in a chain restaurant. No franchises. No common fast food.

"Anders, we're going to see America through local diners, greasy dives, neighborhood bistros, and mom-and-pop cafés. We're eating regional cuisine. We'll order chicken-fried steak from servers with twangs and with stories to tell." I could taste it.

"All right, Dad," Anders said, momentarily looking up from the computer screen after buying another pair of tickets. "But only chain hotels."

"Deal."

After the five Coreys paid homage once more to Fenway, Anders and I began the road trip. In Mullica Hill, New Jersey, we ordered breast of chicken francaise and linguini with hot sausage at the Harrison House Diner and Restaurant, one of the many shiny-chromed Garden State eateries marking the state's restaurant culture. We wondered aloud what made the Harrison House a diner *and* a restaurant.

Judy came to our table, fiftysomething and aproned.

"Hi, Judy," I said. "I'm Barry and this is my son Anders. We're on a cross-country road trip, father and son. Got a new job in California. We're driving coast to coast."

Anders, for the first time of many, rolled his eyes and looked away. Judy, like the many strangers my father befriended throughout his life, indulged my cheerfulness.

"Welcome to the Harrison House Diner and Restaurant!" I was happy to be welcomed to both.

The New Jersey Turnpike yielded to I-95 through Philadelphia and Baltimore before we arrived in Washington. Washington Nationals versus Cincinnati Reds, July 31. At the end of the game, it was 6–3, Washington.

We drove south through Virginia, eating local burgers at Lynchburg's misnamed Texas Inn, settling into two of its fifteen stools. It seemed like neither an inn nor Texas. Charlotte Knights versus Toledo Mud Hens, August 1. Mud Hens won 2–1. A blown tire later, we arrived in Georgia. Atlanta Braves versus Houston Astros, August 2. The Braves lost 11–12 in a fourteen-inning hitters' display.

After a short night's sleep, the next morning's Hampton Inn wake-up call was like reveille jolting us up at dawn. Heading due west on I-20, we saw the Atlanta skyline disappear in our rearview mirror and Alabama appear in our sights. Roll Tide. It was one of five states I'd never entered.

By the time the trip was done, I was down to three. I checked each new state off our list.

By day four, the pattern was predictable. Early-morning drives were low on talk. Anders stared out the window while I drove, reminding myself that conversations with teenage boys before noon often generate guttural replies.

Finally, I broke the silence. "Ever hear of Bear Bryant, legendary coach of Alabama football?" I asked Anders, the boy of all things sports.

"Uh-uh," he said, the opposite of his morning "uh-huh."

I'd fix that. We pulled off at exit 73 and drove a few miles north, parking the Volvo in an empty spot outside Rama Jama's. The café was not much to look at from the outside, but it fit our nonchain conditions. The University of Alabama's 102,000-seat Bryant-Denny Stadium was just a first down away from where we parked, dwarfing the dive's small wooden frame. The Rama Jama's sign on its outside wall was bait for two American sojourners: "Breakfast. Hamburgers. Hot dogs. Onion Rings. Fries." As far as we were concerned, that period after "breakfast" could just as well have been a colon.

A woman sat alone in a neighboring booth as Anders and I waited for delivery of grits and gravied biscuits.

"Where y'all from?" she asked, detecting our dialect from north of the Mason-Dixon Line.

"Thanks for asking. This is my son Anders. We're on a cross-country road trip, father and son. Got a new job in California. We're driving coast to coast. I'm Barry. You?"

"Ruby. Born and raised in Tuscaloosa. Graduated from the University of Alabama, worked at the school until I retired." She directed our attention to a cemetery across the street. "Both my folks are laid to rest in that graveyard. I've got me a plot too. Welcome to Tuscaloosa. Thanks for visiting our city."

When our story met another's story, it was magical. My heart warmed. Anders's eyes rolled.

After breakfast, we took a quick tour of the football stadium. Before we toured the Paul W. "Bear" Bryant Museum, a student walked up to us with that day's *New York Times* tucked under his arm.

"Excuse me, but are you the father and son on a cross-country road trip because of your new job in California?"

A vain thought entered my mind. We were now the luminaries of Tuscaloosa.

"Yes we are," I said, relishing the fame. "How'd you know?"

"I was in Rama Jama's and overheard your story. It moved me. Called my dad a few minutes ago. Asked him if he'd mind taking me on a road trip, just the two of us."

Anders posed with the student for a picture.

Maybe, though I'm not sure, Anders began to realize this ride was something special. For the rest of the trip, when I gave those curious indulgers my familiar refrain, his eyes rolled less often.

Every time we were about to cross a state line, I'd rouse Anders from his reading or daydreaming and ask him to get out the camera. Alabama. Mississippi. Louisiana. Texas.

Texas took a while to cover. Neither the Rangers nor the Astros were in town, so there was no need to stop except to refill on gas and food.

During the drive, Anders frequently sat in the backseat to read a book or watch episodes of *24* on my laptop. When he wasn't looking, I'd adjust the rearview mirror from pointing out the back window to pointing at my son's face, not unlike when he was in his toddler's seat.

Years later, I was still checking to see if he was all right.

He never noticed me, sometimes because he'd fallen asleep, just as he had on those rides home from Fenway Park when I was thirty-seven and he was six. The years between had evaporated. As we drove westward across the plains and as the East kept disappearing behind us, I thought deeply about this change I'd brought about in our family. I thought about our children, about my towing them, involuntarily, to California. Those were quiet miles as I'd cast my glances at the teenager rapt in his reading or watching or napping, wondering why I'd said yes. And I thought about the uncertainty that I had said yes to.

Abraham obeyed and went, even though he did not know where he was going.

I pondered my ambitions versus Anders's needs. What new world was I forcing on him? I checked and rechecked my soul as the mile markers ticked down, asking myself what I was inflicting on our family in pursuit of my own ambitions. How did I even know my ambitions would work out? What if I failed? It may not be the faithful question, but it was the honest one. My new vocational calling seemed noble and selfish at the same time. Anders and his siblings had no choice. Paula was committed to making this work. I sighed with each glance at Anders through the rearview mirror, decelerating as if to delay the inevitable.

With each new state, the road trip's enchantment waned as layer upon layer of self-doubt, real or perceived, shrouded my spirits. The promise of what lies ahead is never as concrete as the memories of life left behind.

We checked in to a chain hotel in Amarillo, keeping Anders's deal with me. We ate red meat at the Big Texan, keeping my deal with him. Church on Sunday. New Mexico by Sunday night. Albuquerque Isotopes six, Colorado Springs Sky Sox four.

We'd cover Albuquerque to Flagstaff Monday and then the homestretch from Flagstaff to Anaheim on Tuesday. For many miles, our drive paralleled historic Route 66, that ribbon of a highway stretching from Chicago to Santa Monica. Wanting to savor these moments and to put off the destination, I exited the interstate to drive that well-traveled but now abandoned Mother Road, America's Main Street.

"Anders, get in the driver's seat," I said to our barely teenage son as I pulled off at an exit with no services nearby, stopping the car on the ramp's dusty shoulder. The old Route 66, long untraveled with its asphalt cracking, waited for fathers like me to give their sons a rite of passage. We switched seats, and Anders, without once adjusting the mirrors, stepped on the accelerator for his maiden voyage. He barely blinked for those few miles, fiercely gripping the wheel as I sat in the passenger seat, my inner self wrestling with so many simultaneous changes.

The Colorado River separates Arizona from California. On that hot August day when the only visible moisture for miles had been the phantom puddles on the heat-waved interstate, we were about to cross the river and finally enter the state of our destiny.

We'd chronicled our pilgrimage by photographing signs inviting us to the next state. Welcome to Mississippi. Welcome to Louisiana. Welcome to Texas. Welcome to New Mexico. Welcome to Arizona. The next sign was just on the other side of the river. "Get the camera," I bid Anders one last time. "We're about to enter our new home." We crossed the Colorado River, which separated the western desert of Arizona from the eastern desert of California. I slowed the car as he rolled down the window, leaning at just the right angle to frame the shot.

Click. Captured. A scrapbook memory. Moving on.

We'd only gone about a mile beyond the river when I turned to say something to Anders. Tears were cresting his eyelids, tumbling off his cheeks onto his jeans.

"Dad, turn around. Take me back. I don't want to do this."

I knew what he meant, though I'd been suppressing those same apprehensions. We were long gone from that small Boston town we'd left ten days ago. It was the kind of town where folks wore "Life is Good" T-shirts and meant it. No traffic lights. Twenty-five hundred families. A cul-de-sac outside our front yard where neighborhood kids gathered for Wiffle ball and where Mr. Bruce, the mailman, occasionally shifted his Jeep into park to take a few at bats. That same town where I worked, our kids schooled, and good friends lived on nearby streets.

Change is hard.

"Dad," Anders reminded me between sniffs, "you're moving me away from my friends, my school, our house, everything I know. Turn around. I want to go home."

He spoke those tender words while we drove through Needles, California, a lifeless town on a scorching run of desert highway. Welcome to California?

He cried. I cried. I wanted to turn on the windshield wipers to make our grief go away.

All of my transcontinental nostalgia didn't mean squat that day. What had I done? I thought this new job was a calling, but maybe it was just a rung. On mile 3,109 of the journey, our suppressed fears were given voice in a fourteen-year-old's pain, and our voices cracked as we together acknowledged our uncertainty.

Abraham is one of the stars of Hebrews 11, the "hall of fame of faith," with more verses devoted to his story than any other person's. Lost to many readers of Hebrews 11, however, are ten inconspicuous words. Abraham obeyed and went, "even though he did not know where he was going" (verse 8). Read: uncertainty.

This has to be among the most honest but glossed-over lines in the sacred Scriptures. Even though Abraham obeyed

God and went, the writer of Hebrews says Abraham didn't have a clue about the journey ahead. And he owned up to the fact that he didn't.

Stop and ponder that for a moment. This isn't just Abraham's line. It's *your* line. It's *my* line.

Who hasn't been there, the place where life is so uncertain we don't know where we're going? We don't know what's next? And we want to hide behind the facade that we *do* know where we're going, that we're certain about life. Or we want to turn around and go back to where life is safe and familiar.

I could think of only one thing to say to my son at that weepy moment as we passed the Needles city limit and headed deeper into the desert: "The Red Sox are in Anaheim tonight, and we'll be there in a few hours."

Anders blinked hard. "Keep driving, Dad," he blubbered. It was as if I had asked him to sell his soul for a bowl of pottage.

I know what he meant. And the truth is, I cried not just because I was sad, but because I was scared. Sure, I'd been disguising it behind half-feigned stories of adventure on the journey and heartstringed lines about fathers and sons and the trip of a lifetime. But the fear was real.

What troubled Anders and me was not the loss of the life we'd left behind but the uncertainty of the unknown life to come. For some, uncertainties are opiates: the more unknown, the bigger the thrill. Not for me. Not for my son. And not for most.

Hebrews 11:8-10 is the *SparkNotes* of Genesis, the narrative of patriarchs Abraham, Isaac, and Jacob and their clans.

It illustrates a truth we see consistently throughout Scripture and in our own lives: people of God on the journey are not at all certain about what's next, whether it's the journey from Ur to Hebron or Boston to LA.

My life on that road trip had been rife with uncertainty. Would our New England house sell in a tanking real estate market? Did I have what it took to be the president of a university way larger than any place I'd ever worked? Would our children make new friends? The *right* friends? Would the trauma of moving take its toll on their decisions? On our marriage? What if I was fired or quit in desperation? What would we do with our snow shovels?

Our joyride had become joyless at that moment in the desert. We'd given up the "Life is Good" life in Boston, and we couldn't turn back.

Life is a journey from certainty to uncertainty. My story is about a cross-country move and a road trip. Someone else's story of uncertainty may be about the claustrophobia of a dead-end job, or the loneliness of empty nesting, or the diagnosis that redirects her life, or the tragedy he didn't see coming, or the money that's running thin.

Sometimes we cross the Colorado River and want to turn around, returning to the familiar. We think the antidote to uncertainty is certainty. It's not.

By faith Abraham, when called to go to a place he would later receive as his inheritance, obeyed and went, even though he did not know where he was going.

As our car hummed westward on I-40, I knew the road

and the destination, but I truly didn't know where I was going. I didn't know the bumps in the road that awaited us. I didn't know how my unanswered questions would be resolved. I even wondered if I'd fail.

I didn't have a whole lot of certainty the closer we got to the Pacific Ocean. If certainty means I know what will happen next, I didn't. We don't.

I *wanted* certainty. I wanted to know it would all turn out okay: the job, the kids, the marriage, the friendships. But if certainty means I know what will happen next, then I'm out of luck, because I don't, and I can't.

The cross-country problem for me became this: If the antidote to uncertainty is not certainty, then what is it? How do we, the people of God who are living in uncertainty, respond if certainty is never an option?

Here is what I have discovered and what I am still figuring out. The antidote to uncertainty is not certainty. It's confidence.

In God's metanarrative of grace, there is a world of difference between certainty and confidence. Certainty means I know what will happen next, and I don't. I might have an idea and make my plans accordingly, but the truth is I really do not know what is coming next. Some seasons of my life I'm even more aware of these uncertainties than others.

But confidence means I *trust* what will happen next. The word *confidence, con* plus *fides*, means "with faith." We journey by faith and not by sight. Abraham set out not knowing where he was going, the book of Hebrews inconspicuously notes. But his encounter with uncertainty on the journey becomes understandable when we get to verse 10. Abraham didn't know the road he was taking, but he knew his destination: the city God built. The American storyteller Eudora Welty writes in her book *One Writer's Beginnings*, "Writers and travelers are mesmerized alike by knowing of their destinations."[1] Knowing your destination does not always mean knowing how you'll get there.

Living a life of radical kindness, a life that others are watching, means owning up to the fact that our lives are messy and uncertain, our roads are crooked. We don't have it all together. The kind life acknowledges that we have little true certainty, a claim that seems so countercultural. The wonder in which we live as people of the Spirit is that the wind of the Spirit—as the Gospel of John says—"blows wherever it pleases. You hear its sound, but you cannot tell where it comes from or where it is going. So it is with everyone born of the Spirit" (3:8). It blows without our logic and where it pleases. As my home church pastor said, "God is totally reliable but hardly predictable."

When I was a lot younger, I heard an old preacher give a sermon that has been lost to time. But one of his lines stuck in my mind: "The eight most dangerous words in the English language are 'I've got to get control of my life.'" The life that seems to be in control is not the kind, honest life. We gain control by relinquishing control. We allow ourselves to decrease so Christ in us can increase. That's when the aroma of Christ wafts around us instead of our own stink.

The life of kindness is the *authentic* life—not the perfect life, and not the predictable life, and hardly the buttoned-up life. It is the life that accepts uncertainties and responds with confidence. The way of kindness is far more about truthfulness than it is the myth of having it all together. I have often hidden behind the simple answers to the messy, complex uncertainties I encounter. H. L. Mencken said, "There is always a well-known solution to every human problem— neat, plausible, and wrong."[2]

To lean into kindness means honestly embracing our limitations and fears, that we do not have this road trip all figured out. The world is watching our response to bumps on the road that shake our chassis and to potholes that bust our axle. Those on the outside of our faith want to see how we respond to the hardships and sufferings. To them, our propped-up perfection doesn't mean diddly.

My own instincts are to live in a way that implies to others that I have my future plotted and my life just right. The way of kindness removes, or at least lowers, the mask. It's not necessarily a life of transparency, which means everything can be seen. But it is at least a life of translucency, where we let light shine through ourselves that reveals the messiness in which we all journey.

It's okay if we don't know where we're going (uncertainty) so long as we know what we're looking for (confidence). Abraham didn't know where he was going, but a few verses later the Scriptures acknowledge what he was looking for, keeping his eyes fixed on a city that has foundations, "whose architect and builder is God" (Hebrews 11:10). Or what the writer says in the beginning of the next chapter: "We . . . [keep] our eyes on Jesus" (12:2, NLT). Though sometimes through the windshield the road looks twisted, in the rear-view mirror it somehow all becomes straight. The journey makes more sense in retrospect.

The bumper sticker I saw while writing this chapter (a nod to J. R. R. Tolkien) captured the idea of confidence: "Not all who wander are lost." It's okay to pass through the wandering seasons of life when we don't know where we're going, so long as we know what we're looking for, keeping our eyes fixed on Christ.

I wonder what the poet had in mind in the longest of all psalms with the words "Your word is a lamp for my feet, a light on my path" (Psalm 119:105). Maybe the psalmist means we have fearful days when we cannot see more than one step at a time, and we need that lamp to shine on our feet. We need the light to guide us day by day, even hour by hour, because that's how far we can see. The voice of God leads us step by step when the rest of our life looks so dark. And maybe the idea of the Word of God as a light to our path assures us during those days when the way is straight, the road is less bumpy. Sometimes we have a clear path for the light of God's Word to guide us. And sometimes we can see no farther than our feet below us.

Living in confidence means that though on the journey we may be afraid, we are not alone.

Anders's first few years in California were sometimes as

desolate as Needles. He struggled through high school, lacked motivation, and was easily distracted. Instead of focusing on his studies, he holed up in his room with his *ESPN* magazine. I wondered about my wisdom at the river, driving on despite my son's pleas to return home.

But over time, the crooked road has become straight, as both the prophet Isaiah and Jesus promise. As I look at the messiness from another perspective farther down the road, it has become beautiful, a lot like a tapestry, which from the back looks like a bunch of ugly knots but from the front is a beautiful work of art. Anders is a thriving young man today with good friends, a deepening faith, and an inquisitive mind. That's not always the story of the journey—crooked roads sometimes straighten over a long span of time, and sometimes they only make sense in the eternal panorama.

Like our 3,357-mile baseball adventure, life is an uncertain journey. But if we fix our eyes on the city with foundations, whose architect and builder is God, the adventure is infused with joy. Uncertainty is less debilitating when we meet it *con fides*—with faith—"confident of this, that he who began a good work in [us] will carry it on to completion until the day of Christ Jesus" (Philippians 1:6).

As one modern version of the Scriptures puts Isaiah 43, "Forget about what's happened; don't keep going over old history. Be alert, be present. I'm about to do something brand-new. It's bursting out! Don't you see it? There it is! I'm making a road through the desert, rivers in the badlands." (verses 18-19, MSG).

Don't you see it? Put on your cleats and step up to bat. Hop in the family car and follow that road to the Promised Land, even if it takes you through the desert. It's time to go through the open door with confidence. When people see us living this way, acknowledging uncertainty but meeting it with faith, we are living a life of profound kindness.

Chapter 3

THE SECURITY OFFICER ON DAY ONE: THE WAY OF KINDNESS LOOKS LIKE HUMILITY

[God] gives us more grace. That is why Scripture says:
"God opposes the proud but shows favor to the humble."
—JAMES 4:6

No one told me during my interviews for this job that the president had to have an arm. The contract with the Los Angeles Dodgers had been signed months earlier as part of the university's centennial, committing the incoming president—whoever she or he would be—to throw the first pitch at a home game.

After moving our family to California, it wasn't long before I found myself standing at various podiums giving speech after speech. The new speeches I gave, one after another, were nothing compared to the anxiety I felt about the coming moment on the mound at Dodger Stadium. For weeks I kept a catcher's mitt nearby for anyone who wanted to be on the receiving end of my practice pitches. An infielder for the university's baseball squad met me several times on the lawn outside the administration building to give me pitching tips as he patiently scooped up my low hurls or lunged for the ones that went wide. Most were one or the other. Maybe one in five was a strike.

When I arrived with my family at Dodger Stadium, passing through the many permissions to get me to the field, my throat went dry. Walking onto the edge of the diamond for the pregame announcements, I looked up to the bleachers of cheering Biola students, throngs of them. Our university's baseball coach squatted behind home plate as the announcer and the Jumbotron cameraman focused on me. Warm-up pitches were prohibited.

"All I can say, Dad, is you better reach home plate," Anders reminded me more than once as I prepared for my one shot at throwing out a first pitch at a Major League Baseball game. "If you don't, people will think you're the kind of leader that will run the university into the dirt."

Grady Little, the former Red Sox manager, was in the dugout, now captaining the Dodgers. As Anders accompanied me to the mound, he pointed him out, as he also pointed to other erstwhile Red Sox waiting for my pitch, players like Derek Lowe and Bill Mueller. Shea Hillenbrand and Nomar Garciaparra were also there, each a former Red Sox now wearing Dodger blue. Tommy Lasorda stood at the third-base line and later posed with me for a photo, and Vin Scully called the game on that beautiful Sunday in Los Angeles, September 16, 2007.

"Throwing out the first pitch," boomed the cue from the stadium's speakers, "is Barry Corey, president of Biola University, which started one hundred years ago in downtown Los Angeles."

I went for it, telling myself throughout the windup not to one-hop the ball to home plate, which I was naively convinced would be a long-recalled memory for the fans. Instead, I erred on the high side, releasing the ball early. The university coach crouching behind the plate did all he could to leap up, catching the errant high ball before it soared over his outstretched glove. At least it didn't squib into the dirt. But it was far from the blistering fastball in the strike zone I'd practiced countless times in my imagination. No radar guns tracked my toss, and the Dodgers' staff quickly whisked me off the field for the real throwing to begin.

I don't know why I cared so much about throwing the perfect pitch. Actually, I do know why. I wanted the crowds to be impressed with the talents I possessed. Most weren't even watching, let alone caring.

The way of kindness is often the way of self-effacement, not mounting high horses or being hung up on perfection. People are far more receivable when they don't take themselves too seriously, when they can laugh at themselves and shrug off their shortcomings.

The challenge accompanying the life of kindness is that it calls us to the way of the meek and not the way of the proud. Pride gives us a shield to hide behind. Meekness exposes our weaknesses. It is the difficult but healthier road to follow.

The fact is, being president of a university gets me a lot of attention, most of it undeserved. I act like I don't like the fawning, but most of the time I do. I avoid introducing myself to others by saying I'm the president. But usually I hope they'll ask. And when I tell them my job, I await their "wow" response—maybe wanting to take a picture with me or to know more about my important role, what presidents do. When I catch myself having these thoughts, something in me feels slimy.

The kinder way is to be present in others' lives with an honest spirit that isn't waiting for the conversation to turn toward me. That's a spirit that receives others more than it wants to be received. One of my friends said that when he walks into a room, he doesn't want to be thinking, *Here I am*. He wants to be thinking, *There you are*. That is the way of kindness, but it's a difficult path for those like me who at our best say we're competitive and at our worst realize how pompous we truly are.

When it was announced I was chosen as president of Biola University, my Puerto Rican friend in Boston began calling me *el presidente*. Those who'd long given me only passing notice began to chat like we were old friends. My banal jokes were suddenly funny. When acquaintances stopped me to talk, flattery frequently followed. I, the five-foot-nine educational bureaucrat, had bypassed a few rungs on the career ladder and landed the CEO spot. Nice.

When the congratulations came, I feigned "aw shucks" humility. It's a feigning, unfortunately, I've learned to master.

As I externally deflected conversations away from my accomplishment, I internally begged for the conversation to stay about me. I wanted to do the humble brag. It's a vice, I know. On more than one occasion I successfully manipulated the small talk back to my new presidential title. I knew my mother would be proud. That was a given. But in my more depraved moments, I wanted everyone to be proud of me, and to say so.

Letters of felicitations arrived in my in-box and my mailbox. Press releases scattered far and wide. I bound the letters and releases in a book. This was a big move to a big job at a big university in a big state with a big team. I'd read and reread them, always when no one was looking. What we do when no one is looking is a dead giveaway of our character.

In the Gospel of Matthew, before Jesus starts into his "woe to you" admonitions, he cautions religious leaders like me who "love to be greeted with respect in the marketplaces and to be called 'Rabbi' by others" (Matthew 23:7). Or "president."

Just days before I arrived in the Golden State and a few weeks before I returned to Boston for the road trip with Anders, my predecessor in the presidency enjoyed a royal and appropriate send-off. After twenty-five years in the seat into which I'd soon park myself, this gentle and inimitable leader walked out of his office for the last time as chief. The staff asked him to don his academic regalia for the curtain call. The president's bride of fifty years held his arm, and the first couple's recessional took them through the office suites, down the staircase, across the yard, and to their waiting car.

Scores of loyal and admiring employees flanked the walkways, extending their ovations through loud cheers and clapping hands. It was deserved pageantry.

When I, the newly heralded president, showed up the next week, things were different. Nobody was flanking anything.

Driving a Ford Taurus rental car from Long Beach Airport to the campus that hot summer day, I answered my ringing cell phone. "Dr. Corey, this is campus safety. Before you get here, we wanted to give you a heads-up. The air-conditioning is not working today. The administration building has no power."

I hoped this wasn't a metaphor.

"Oh, and it's Fourth of July weekend, sir," the officer continued. "The place is basically empty."

That is what the sergeant said, but *this* is what I heard: "Barry, if you are fanning the flames of hope that a welcome party's awaiting you"—which perhaps I was—"put down the bellows."

He was right. By the time I parked my car and walked across that lonesome campus, any hopes of an imperial hello to match my predecessor's imperial good-bye evaporated in the California scorch. When I stepped on campus, no one was waving pennants. No one was cheering. No one was even there.

A few old college friends came to meet me, extending their exhortations and blessing me into this new role. We walked into the office with its fresh nameplate, mounted eye level: "Barry H. Corey, President." I acted like I neither noticed nor cared. Truth is, I noticed *and* cared.

Inside the office, the three of us read Scripture and told tales and prayed in the sauna heat. I recall my two friends' heartfelt intercessions. "Dear God, may Barry begin this job with peace, confidence, and humility." One of the two stopped at Albertsons supermarket on the way to campus and bought a small bottle of Bertolli extra virgin olive oil to anoint me into the office and to anoint the office into me. After the dabbing, I put the bottle on my shelf, where it remains today. It was a sacred moment.

Once we completed this modest and impromptu rite, we went out for the new president's welcome party at a local Mexican restaurant. The two of them welcomed the one of me. We small talked while spooning our salty chips into the guacamole. Congratulations, *el presidente*.

The next morning, a Saturday, I got out of bed in my friend's basement, where I'd be living for a few weeks, and headed to the Office of the President, my new vocational cradle.

I was still on Boston time, so early came early that day. I opened the Starbucks at half past five, and within a few minutes I turned on my blinker entering the university gate. It was a ghost town. The campus roads still new to me, I took at least one corrective U-turn as I twisted my way across that deserted cluster of residence halls and classroom buildings and science labs and athletic fields.

But I was not alone. Tailing me was another car, making it pretty much the two of us in that morning campus rush hour.

By the time I pulled my rental car into a visitor's parking

spot, I could see more clearly the profile of the other car. Blue lights on its roof and reflective decal letters on its side revealed that following me was the university's finest: a campus safety patrolman.

My uber-ego soared as I realized one of my job perks would be daily police escort service to my parking space. *Now we're talking.* I stepped out of the car into the dawn darkness to greet the silhouette of the officer, a yellow Taser on his hip and legs slightly spread. All I recall were his words and their tone.

"Get back in the car."

I got it. He was a funnyman messing with me. I laughed. He didn't.

"Get back in the car. Shut the door. Roll down the window."

At that point I decided to comply, even though he worked for me. Submitting to the patrolman's mandate, I slowly returned to the seat I'd just vacated and placed my coffee back in the cup holder.

"You here for a conference or something?"

"No, sir, it's my first day on the job. I'm going to work."

"You ran a stop sign."

"I didn't see it."

"Rolled right through."

"Sorry."

"We take California traffic laws seriously here. From now on, you follow the traffic laws on campus, you hear?"

"Yes, sir."

After a few more seconds of silence, during which time

I ruled out title-dropping, I asked him if I could get out of the car. He gave me permission, and I walked away, dodging a bullet, so to speak.

About an hour later as I rummaged through boxes left for me in the office of the CEO, acting like I was on top of things, *el presidente*, I heard a knock on the door beside my nameplate. Standing before me was the second uniformed and holstered officer I'd seen that day.

"You get pulled over about an hour ago?"

"Yes, sir. I ran a stop sign inadvertently. I won't do it again. How'd you know?"

"I'm the shift supervisor. When I arrived, an officer was writing up a report on the incident."

They called it an *incident*?

The shift supervisor continued. "I asked my partner who he pulled over, and he said something about a guy here for his first day on the job and about setting him straight about traffic laws at the university."

He wasn't done. "I wondered who it was, suspecting perhaps . . . So I opened the university's home page and asked him if the guy he gave what for looked anything like this guy on the website. The reporting officer put down his pen and said, 'Yeah, it looks a lot like him.'"

He works at Home Depot now.

The gist of the story is true, except for the Home Depot part.

I learned a few big lessons day one on the big job. First, the employees at this new place where I work take their jobs *really*

seriously. That's a good thing. Second, the previous day my
two friends prayed I would begin this job with humility, and
the Good Lord answered their prayer in no time flat. I'd soon
enjoy all the pomp and perks of being a college president,
but I needed to enjoy them with the humility God intended.
Sure, I'd get to throw out a first pitch, but I also planned to
heed every stop sign between my office and Dodger Stadium.

Not long after I arrived at my new job, a faculty member
I respect dearly sent me a letter. He reminded me that this
university is not filled with a bunch of egos each trying to
out-publish or out-teach one another, going on to say that
professors take their teaching, scholarship, and care for students with far more earnestness than they take themselves.
I read between the lines that those who teach here are more
interested in building a community than a pedestal.

I took the wise professor's letter as a personal dose of
advice, especially the caution against triumphalism, which
can be my default. He exhorted:

> Biola University . . . is not a collective prima
> donna. There may be individual exceptions, but
> on the whole we don't take ourselves too seriously,
> but we take God's calling on our lives with deadly
> seriousness. So we won't have a huge agenda for you
> to fulfill, but rather will pray that God's giftedness
> in your life will help facilitate God's vision for all of
> us. I weary of hearing schools trying to become the
> greatest or the best; when that kind of comparative

competition exists, someone always loses, which means the Kingdom of God loses effectiveness. I sense that we just want to be faithful as stewards of the gospel of the Kingdom of God. And I sense the same of you. That, I trust, will help you to relax.

That professor's letter and the safety officer's admonition were caution signs to me: *Get over your ego.* The title I was given as president could vaporize even faster than I got it. The maintenance worker could unscrew and replace the nameplate beside the president's door as just one more work order. I'm learning that leaning into the way of kindness means accepting the fact that position is less meaningful than posture. Performance is less effective than purpose. Pretense is less effective than candor. I've seen too many leaders who, like me, devour the attention and grope for the microphone and expect the fawning.

How come the throngs weren't there to greet me? I asked myself on the first day.

"It ain't the heat," Yogi Berra once quipped, "it's the humility."

Too often I see leadership fossilizing kindness. It's not that leaders don't have the spirit of kindness within us. It's just that it is buried under too many layers of pressures or prestige we carry every day. "Lord," I often pray, "make my heart kind." One of the most difficult challenges of being a leader is to keep fresh a sense of loving-kindness. It's often suppressed by my sense of entitlement.

We become amnesiac about what John, Jesus' forerunner, said about posture: "Christ must increase and I must decrease" (see John 3:30). My proclivity is to say, "I must increase, and then I think I'll increase some more." The thirst for self-importance is not easily quenched. Kindheartedness the way Jesus describes it, however, demands a shrunken me. "Whoever receives you receives me," Jesus said, "and whoever receives me receives him who sent me" (Matthew 10:40, ESV). My prayer is that I don't stop this phrase after the first pronoun in the "whoever receives you" part.

May I make myself receivable—kindhearted—not because of the title I hold or the seat I occupy, not because I'm a recognized face or a Googleable name. May I walk the way of kindness because of the Christ I love, whose aroma I carry. May I learn that a lesson in life is a lessened me. May the proportions of Christ in me wax as my ego wanes. When civility and humility stop being marks of a Christian, the salt has lost its savor and the light has been hidden under a bushel.

In her powerful and precious novel *Gilead*, Marilynne Robinson gets at this through her story's speaker, the parson and dad: "When the Lord says you must 'become as one of these little ones,' I take Him to mean you must be stripped of all the accretions of smugness and pretense and triviality."[1]

As I read the story in John 3 when Nicodemus, the come-by-night Pharisee, flattered Jesus with his welcoming words, I hear what is so often my own buttering-up voice: "Rabbi, we know that you are a teacher who has come from God. For no one could perform the signs you are doing if God were not with him" (verse 2). But Jesus didn't need the fawning. Instead, he bypassed the praise about his reputation and declared back to the fawner, "Very truly I tell you, no one can see the kingdom of God unless they are born again" (verse 3).

Christ "did not count equality with God something to be grasped, but made himself nothing, taking the very nature of a servant" (Philippians 2:6-7). He did this so that the people of God, like the Philippian church Paul was addressing, might begin to understand what true Jesus community looks like, feels like, smells like. I want to write my narrative as I go forward so that it's a story line that doesn't read like my résumé.

Humility leads to harmony.

I struggle with this because I'm competitive. I have the tendency to talk about where "my university" is ranked or the good things luminaries like Mark Noll or Bill Bennett are saying about us. My depravity sometimes sees other universities' struggles as our getting the upper hand, as if we are somehow more spiritual and therefore more blessed. May God convict me of *that* version of a prosperity doctrine. If we are to be effective in our culture *and* in the long run, we need to resist the temptation toward conceit.

I am regularly bothered by the instinctive language I hear myself using in describing the university where I work, inserting definers that end in "e-s-t" or adjectives like *exemplary, renowned, leading, significant, model*, and *world-class*. Are these descriptors *true*? I believe they are, or at least we're aspiring for them to be. But I'll leave that for those on the outside to say rather than describing ourselves that way. We must be a city on a hill whose light shines outward and not a city on a hill with the spotlight on ourselves.

Humility does not diminish my desire that we as followers of Jesus strive toward the highest levels of excellence. But we will reach those levels as we pay more attention to words like *faithful, courageous, focused, prudent, integral, honest, prayerful, pensive, learning, Christ-honoring,* and *kind.*

May the position with which I've been entrusted model the words of Jeremiah 9:23-24:

> Let not the wise boast of their wisdom or the strong
> boast of their strength or the rich boast of their
> riches, but let the one who boasts boast about this:
> that they have the understanding to know me, that
> I am the LORD, who exercises kindness, justice and
> righteousness . . . for in these I delight.

Justice and righteousness are the virtues that accompany kindness. May these be my default.

One of several moments I still revisit from interviewing for this new job in California happened in a packed auditorium with people lobbing questions my way. I was at that point a finalist for the job, though the board of trustees had not yet voted. The attention all week was over the top, good and otherwise. No stones were left unturned. The questions came one after another at what seemed to be a dizzying interrogation. And I began to descend from my fleeting thoughts of president-to-be self-importance as the grueling grilling went on. I began to weary. Was this job really for me? Would I even succeed if invited? Did I really need and want to be a university president? If I couldn't handle the hot seat of the interview, how would I handle the hot seat of the role?

As the room emptied after the hour lapsed, one university student came up to me with a folded piece of paper, slipping it into my hands before walking away. I can't recall what he even looked like, but I can't forget what the note said:

> Dr. and Mrs. Corey, Thousands have been praying
> for you, none have taken this lightly. Welcome here.
> Please, live simply that we may have an example
> to follow. Give us Jesus. Keep us urgent. Ask for
> patience, especially within your first two years here.
> Don't let us stay inside the bubble. Take us outside for
> the Kingdom of God. Eat in the cafeteria often. Know
> your students. Be hospitable. Love us dearly. Love one
> another before us. Love Him so much more. Fiercely
> guard what we stand for. Do not glorify us. We do
> not need expensive pretty things, we want to be wise,
> practical, and to give it all to our Lord. Remember
> beauty for ashes. Be encouraged. Welcome here.

At that low point in the interview week, I began to look up. I thought then, and have thought since, that if this is the character of students studying here, this is where I need to be. This is where I'm called. Years later, that letter is still tucked in my Bible. It reminds me of the sacred trust I have been given in this position and not some nameplate on my door.

I have days when nothing is going right. A parent is angry or a proposal is rejected or a speech I gave flopped. And I feel like I'm failing as a leader. During those low moments I am convinced I've fooled them all into thinking I am worthy of the title. My self-esteem plummets.

And I have days when the university's on a roll and I revel in my self-importance that it's all because of me. Our enrollment goals are met or students high-five me walking along the campus sidewalk or fund-raising is over the top. During these headier times I convince myself I'm leading invincibly, smugly thinking how lucky everyone is to have me in charge. My self-esteem rockets.

But both are unhealthy places: allowing my self-esteem to plummet or to rocket. When I hang out too long in either place, I feel the destructive forces of self-berating or self-inflating, one or the other. God in his mercy calls me to sobering reminders like that student's letter, beckoning me again to "live simply that they may have an example to follow" and to "give them Jesus." And this is the calling that keeps me centered when I'm feeling either failure or swagger. My calling is to rise above my own self-inflicted scorn or my own standing ovation and be content in my holy calling, the healthy place where we all need to rest. This is a place where hope sprouts and fear subsides and meekness coexists with leadership. And it's a place where loving others in a spirit of kindness comes more naturally.

I've got a few "endgame" commitments for when I retire from this job or when I'm shown the door. I want to make sure my spiritual life doesn't tailspin because somehow I've morphed my title with my calling, mistaking being president of the university with being resident in Christ. God, protect me from confusing what I do with who I am. With all of the attention in Christian leadership on God-this and God-that, I can quickly be hypnotized into equating my job description with my spiritual condition. This is a dangerous place to be, where ego and vanity seep into spiritual identity. When this happens, I've essentially slammed the door on living the way of kindness.

I believe I'm good at what I do. But I am in this role not because I'm good but because I'm called. As soon as I forget this, I'll begin to fantasize again about all of the attention I deserve, the nameplate on the door of my office, and all of the applause I am owed as *el presidente*.

Chapter 4

THE GAY CONVERSATION IN DHAKA: THE WAY OF KINDNESS WHEN WE DISAGREE

The Word became flesh and made his dwelling among us.
We have seen his glory, the glory of the one and only Son,
who came from the Father, full of grace and truth.

—JOHN 1:14

Our conversation wandered without logic through some of this and some of that before Karen said, "I haven't told you, but I'm in a relationship back in the States with a seminary student."

"Tell me about him," I instinctively replied.

Karen corrected my pronoun, which was the very reason she wanted to talk that day. "I'll tell you about *her.*"

Despite my theological convictions, I was one of the first people Karen told about her lesbian relationship.

Kindness calls us to enter conversations with those whose perspectives differ from ours. But sometimes in our zeal for a firm center, we default to lectures from the sidelines rather than initiating gracious conversations with those whose standards are different, sometimes far different, from our own. When we respond this way, our edges calcify, and grace is lost in a fight for truth. In these situations, firm centers with firm edges rarely work. This approach leads to wall building, not bridge building. Soft centers with soft edges won't work either. It leaves us adrift like a rudderless boat.

In Jesus' way of kindness, we can be confident in our beliefs and also comfortable listening to those with differing views. Anyone who lives this way of kindness will find a path to share the truth of God's will and grace as we see it in Scripture.

The point of being kind to those with whom we disagree is not to be respected or befriended. That may never happen. Nor is the point of kindness to avoid either ruffling feathers or feeling awkward, which is cowardly "niceness." The point of kindness is to represent Jesus. Being kind to those with whom we disagree helps bring Christ to the center of the situation. Being kind is how Jesus acts. Kindness is his way. When we walk that way, we reflect and honor him, and it opens doors for what we say about him and the gospel.

This is not to say that we "use" kindness as a tactic or treat those with whom we interact as a means to some further end. That's not the way of Jesus. To honor Jesus is to live and love as he does. With kindness that is genuine and winsome and with love that is unconditional and relentless, we are able to love people where they are. We are able to point them to their greatest good, which is found only in the gospel.

Today, there's no issue more likely to distract the church from its mission, to divide us as Christians and to separate us from the culture, than how we respond in the face of changing attitudes on same-sex relationships and marriage. It is also the issue that more than any other will test the way of kindness. The velocity of change in the public's perception of same-sex relationships is staggering. What does a firm center and soft edges look like in the gay conversation?

It looks a lot different than it did when I was growing up.

When it came to anything gay, in my family it was hush, in my church it was harsh, and in my neighborhood it was a joke. That sums up my childhood and adolescent perspective on all things LGBT (lesbian, gay, bisexual, transgender) and sometimes Q (for questioning or queer). To me, those four or five letters had no meaning at all.

As a boy growing up in the Corey home, I have no recollection of conversations about gay issues other than whispers and innuendo. Nor was homosexuality talked about in my church, other than being cited by traveling evangelists as among the moral abominations they rattled off in a fire-breathing sermon. Around my boyhood friends, we skirted the subject except for our repartee of one-liners, each quip reaffirming our masculinity. To this day, I have no idea who was laughing only on the outside.

Not long into my first semester at a Midwestern Christian college, age eighteen and halfway across the country, word on the floor spread that a few of my residence hall neighbors were same-sex attracted, or at least sexually experimenting that way. Caught, they were expelled in a matter of days for violating the community's covenant on sexual behavior. These young men began repacking the boxes that a few months earlier they'd unpacked. From the dorm windows a jeerer or two lobbed undignified and derogatory epithets as our former classmates loaded their cars, their academic careers at this college summarily terminated.

Expulsion didn't temper the insensitive slurs, mine or anyone else's. Life went on among the reinstated heterosexual collegiate halls, purged of anyone oriented otherwise. At least that's what the subculture wanted and what we assumed.

One college friend and classmate came out around the time he graduated, before heading to work as an accountant in an East Coast city. Another came out a few years later and is now on the West Coast in a same-sex marriage and has a child. Yet another headed to a career in theater, out as well. Some of us wondered what it was in their genetics or what happened in their childhoods that made them gay, speculating ignorantly on this or that. Over time, I lost contact with those college acquaintances, hearing only through grapevines where they lived and in some cases with whom. Occasionally I considered reaching out and then did nothing, telling myself our worlds were different. Our circles no longer overlapped. Life was busy, and many college friendships naturally go dormant.

Toward them, my edges were firm. Perhaps even hard.

What would we talk about? I wasn't sure we could get beyond the fact that I believe the paradigm of marriage is between one man and one woman, a union modeled in Scripture that has withstood millennia and has been the norm in all kinds of cultures. We could be civil and reminisce about old friends, but then what? Would they think my ideas archaic because I've read and reread the Scriptures, understanding sexual intimacy outside of marriage—straight, gay, or otherwise—as beyond God's intention? Would I be thought of as an intolerant bigot, out of step and hateful?

As to reconnecting with old friends who have come out, I resorted to asking, "Why bother?"—uncomfortable with that perspective but without the bandwidth for the alternatives. I realize it's a pathetic response.

After college and during my occasional wonderings about these erstwhile classmates, I moved to Dhaka, Bangladesh, to see the world and to find myself, then lost in my own crisis of "normalcy." I had long enjoyed my cozy world of a cherished family, a decent education, and a handful of great friends. Growing up was rather trauma free. No one close to me died. My parents paid their credit card bills on time. We weren't evicted. No one close to me had a debilitating injury or sickness. I never had to close my eyes and plug my ears because of things happening at home. My mother never took off. My father never philandered. Pans didn't fly, and dishes didn't break. No secondhand smoke, and not even a jug of wine. In all this normalcy—halfway through my graduate studies at Boston College—I left the familiar in order to shake things up, to test my spiritual grit.

My year as a researcher in Southeast Asia at a large non-governmental organization plunged me into the unfamiliar—exactly what my all-too-normal self wanted. Abject poverty was ubiquitous. People I'd long known about but never knew became my colleagues and friends. I shared office space with Muslims and Hindus, and they became my traveling companions during that year of adventure. My handful of new expat chums held passports from Australia and Sweden and Canada and the UK. Along with the unfamiliar Pakistani, Turk, or Sri Lankan I befriended during my year abroad, I also met and befriended the unfamiliar gay and lesbian.

I didn't see it coming.

Karen was a bright and savvy anthropologist and one-time Fulbright Scholar conducting research in Bangladesh. As we'd say in Boston, she was "wicked smaht." We connected because we had the Fulbright thing in common. Karen mastered Bengali and the cultural norm of eating with her right hand rather than with a fork, artfully keeping the food from dripping past her second knuckles. She made friends. I made a mess. I watched as she quickly and disarmingly embraced locals, conversing easily and laughing freely. I envied the receptivity she earned through her language skills and natural graces. She was welcoming, affirming, and bright. Early on, Karen selflessly helped me navigate that strange new world.

Karen and I also saw each other in church on Fridays, the Islamic holy day, when stores and offices closed. The few hundred of us were assembled in our unity despite our nuanced theological diversity, a diversity that reflected the vast number and flavors of our churches. In our home countries, we identified as Presbyterian and Pentecostal, Baptist and Anglican, Reformed and Lutheran. In Dhaka, we identified as Christ-followers, worshiping together and walking side by side to the Lord's Table as the people of God. We gathered as middle-class American researchers and South Korean missionaries and Danish agronomists and embassy workers from African nations. We, the body of Christ—all of us broken—gathered at the international high school as a religious minority in a predominantly Muslim nation.

Karen worshiped too.

One notable midday as I was going about my research on "non-formal primary education for children of the landless poor," Karen came by to see me. The conversation went something like this:

"You want to get some lunch?"

"Okay."

"Good, because I need to talk with you."

"Everything all right, Karen?"

"Let's get some lunch."

Twenty minutes and twenty taka later, we arrived by rickshaw at the American Club, where our coveted membership cards gained us privileged access to a few hectares of the familiar. The walled compound insulated us from Dhaka's noise and beggars and crowds and trash-strewn streets. We drank iced teas and ordered BLTs while Bruce Springsteen's "Born in the U.S.A." played poolside over the speakers.

Karen and I were among the few within shouting distance of the American Club who identified with the Boss's lyrics.

Our conversation wandered before Karen told me about her relationship back home "with a seminary student." I was one of the first people Karen told. At that moment, none of the old homophobic jokes came to mind. My spirit didn't recoil. I didn't look away. Neither did any insulting labels spin through my thoughts.

More than once Karen caught herself saying, "I can't believe I'm making this revelation to you, a conservative pastor's son who is theologically somewhere else." She was right. I was both of those: a pastor's kid and elsewhere theologically. I was and remain anchored by a biblical ethic where same-sex physical intimacy resides outside of God's ideal and intention.

I asked her why she was telling *me*, someone who's obviously straight, at that point engaged to Paula, and neither a trained counselor nor an LGBT ally.

She told me not because she thought I'd agree with her relationship. She wasn't asking me to consider changing my position or becoming an advocate. Karen understood my biblical position on sex even though she interpreted the Scriptures differently. But she told me because she knew if I was living out my faith as a Christian, I'd receive her with grace first, not judgment. She trusted I wouldn't backpedal on my confession that if I love God, I also must love my neighbor as myself. She opened up to me because she believed authentic Christians see all people first and foremost as created in God's image and of immense value. Because Karen knew me, she came out to me, convinced my first response would be kindness. I don't think I let her down.

We talked that day over our two-course American lunch and many times over the course of our year in Bangladesh. I spent time in the home of Karen and her same-sex spouse several years later when I returned to Dhaka. We've had a few conversations since about life and about the journey of relationships. Then for years it all went quiet.

Because I listened to her, I kept Karen's respect. She wasn't asking me to be a cocelebrant, something she knew I could not be. She was asking me to hear her story and to continue as the same friend I was prior to knowing this aspect of her life.

Karen put a face on homosexuality, as well as a voice and a name. What began as a conversation in Dhaka's American Club stayed with me over the years, tempering my edges without tampering with my center. For the first time, I sat across a table and listened to a friend tell me about her same-sex attractions. Before our talk, my knee-jerk responses from a distance might have been to label, prejudge, and make sweeping assumptions. My table-side response over lunch was to hear her story and to begin a long conversation, a conversation I pray honors the righteousness of Christ and respects the honesty of Karen.

How do we live a life with a firm center and soft edges in conversations on human sexuality? What does kindness look like on one of the hot-button issues of our generation? Where do grace and truth cohabit?

Not long after that lunch, a cyclone in the Bay of Bengal tore into Bangladesh's southern coast with fierce winds and tidal waves and power failures. That night in late April 1991, the awful storm killed nearly 140,000 unprepared children, women, and men.

Karen, whose heart is as big as the Indian Ocean, told me she had to help and wanted me to join her. As part of an emergency response relief team, Karen and I boarded an overpacked train destined for the most devastated areas. For several days she and I worked together for the lives of the people shattered by havoc. Our divergent views on matters of sexuality and marriage didn't matter as much as we served people in turmoil. Despite our differences, we worked side by side to alleviate what we both agreed was unconscionable suffering. Karen and I agreed we would minister together among the poor. And we agreed that our biblical views of human sexuality were out of sync.

After I left Bangladesh, our communication waned, and it's been twenty years since we've been in touch. While writing this book and considering the importance of how Christians respond in kindness to those who are gay, I tracked Karen down. This was an initiative I had not taken over the years with my "outed" college friends. Karen and I began to communicate, and I even asked her if I could tell her story in this chapter about why she came out to me, a biblically conservative Christian. She knows—though many others in the gay community may not see it this way—that a biblically conservative follower of Jesus is not the same as a closed-minded, right-wing fanatic. This is a misconception Christians need to work on correcting through their actions, and skeptics of the faith need to open their minds to consider that the two are not the same.

As Christians, we take seriously the idea of *imago Dei*, that God made humans as unique creatures in his image and created us for deep relationships vertically and horizontally. He did this because he is a relational God. Karen still knows I believe the Scriptures are clear on the context for sexual intimacy, and she still knows I admire her deeply as someone made in God's image and loved by him. I'm still learning to understand all the dimensions of people's sexuality, its beauty and its brokenness, mine included. But above all, I desire to be part of God's image-bearing people who relate to each other full of grace and truth, the same way God relates to us through Christ.

Loving those who are different than we are is what we are supposed to do. And we're called to serve together, to eat together, to have long and meaningful conversations with each other, to listen to each other, to sit on pews beside each other. Jesus listened to playful children, promiscuous women, come-by-night religious leaders, corrupt tax collectors, and unclean outcasts.

As I write this chapter, I do so knowing that what I ink will follow me for good or otherwise. Even language labeling can be distracting, and the descriptors we use can become conversation disrupters. At a deeper level, however, the issue is less about labeling from across the street and more about listening from across the table. Listening opens conversations to places these relationships otherwise may not go. And conversations about the deepest issues of our lives are often the places where God's redemptive loving-kindness begins to take root.

I am working on the kindness of listening, understanding more and more the difference between listening while waiting to *respond* to someone and listening while wanting to *learn* about someone. Kindness is the latter. We may disagree on whether and how gay attraction is caused or can change. We may disagree on the context for sexual intimacy. We may disagree on the ideal of marriage. We may disagree on the biblical ethics of sexual conduct. But we should not disagree on whether we begin with kindness, the virtue that invites conversation and calls us to love those from whom we differ.

We don't have conversations for the sake of simply conversing. We also have conversations for the sake of convincing. And convincing takes time and is rarely a one-off. Our conversations as biblically faithful Christians are to convince through friendship and candor, thoughtful articulation and listening, that what we believe is neither mean spirited nor ignorant. We also have conversations in order to be open to learn what we may not have fully understood. Conversations meant both to convince and to learn are at the heart of what it means to be kind. Through listening, we show kindness and respect to those with whom we disagree while at the same time articulating our convictions on the way we believe God intended things to be.

Around the time I was writing this book, the *New York Times* printed a front-page story on a conversation that took place at Biola University, a conversation between differing perspectives on the way Christians with same-sex attraction are called to live out their sexuality. The reporter, who sat in on this conversation, noted in her article that on this issue the vitriol is waning even though for most the convictions are not:

Few are dropping their opposition. But aware that they are seen by many as bigots, some evangelical leaders are trying to figure out how to stand firm without alienating the rising share of Americans— especially younger ones—who know gay people and support gay rights, or who may themselves come out as gay.[1]

I think of conversations I've had with my friend Jim Daly at Focus on the Family, who told me about linking arms with gay rights activists to pass legislation against sex trafficking. The president and CEO of Chick-fil-A, Dan Cathy, countered criticism with kindness by inviting Shane Windmeyer, national director of the LGBTQ group Campus Pride, to a dinner and into a conversation that led to a friendship. It's not much different from the way Karen and I did our small part to bring relief and rice to the ravaged villages on the Bay of Bengal after the cyclone stole life from those communities. Sometimes kindness brings people with different standards together to work for the common good.

Reach-across-the-aisle kindness is not meant to affirm each other's choices, but it does mean we listen to each other's voices. The Jesus way of kindness, because it has a firm center, is at its core a holy kindness. It is kindness rooted in conviction. Kindness does not mean we assent to cultural norms or that we give people a pass to feed their own moral appetites under the guise of individual choice or because "God loves us anyway." God's kind of kindness is far different from niceness or tolerance because it leads us to see his holiness and purity, and from there it leads us to see our own depravity. In Romans 2 Paul writes under the inspiration of the Holy Spirit that kindness will reveal in us and in others our fallen nature and will draw us all to the cross of Christ: "God's kindness is intended to lead you to repentance" (verse 4).

This profound truth about kindness points to its purpose: repentance. God is always yearning for contrite and broken hearts. Kindness, by its nature, can make proud hearts contrite, and this leads to atonement. The nature of God's lovingkindness points toward repentance, and the nature of God's loving-kindness through *us* also points toward repentance. If we live kindly in a "God is kind" way, the unrepentant will be inclined to repent. Kindness helps our relationships begin, and it helps them to endure, relationships that God can use toward transforming lives. Christlike loving-kindness for its own sake is not enough.

But it's not an easy road today for Christian leaders to keep their centers firm *and* their edges soft. Cultural shifts and the intolerance of those who don't respect biblical convictions can cause some people to soften their centers and others to harden their edges. When we want to avoid being perceived as intolerant or hateful, we sometimes roll over and capitulate on our convictions to avoid cultural ire. When we do, we're softening the center. On the other hand, when we are "so angry at those repulsive gays," we can become the pugilists, swinging at everything that threatens our values. Then our edges fossilize. Even though I may believe differently than someone else does, that doesn't mean I don't care about them or can't love them.

As I was writing this book, the United States Supreme Court ruled 5–4 in favor of Obergefell, making gay marriage legal across the nation. How do we respond? The way of kindness calls us to live more than ever with biblical convictions and Christlike love—truth and grace. I pray that thoughtful people of all beliefs will honor and uphold the ideal of pluralism, respecting and defending the rights of religious people and organizations to operate according to the beliefs they hold dear. We must set the example as Christians, standing firm with deep convictions while understanding that our neighbors have the same right to hold beliefs that are different from ours.

As the president of the United States said the morning of the June 2015 Supreme Court decision, "I know that Americans of goodwill continue to hold a wide range of views on this issue. Opposition in some cases has been based on sincere and deeply held beliefs. All of us who welcome today's news should be mindful of that fact; recognize different viewpoints; revere our deep commitment to religious freedom."[2]

As the post–Obergefell decision days unfold, Christians will need to hold confidently their biblical convictions and engage compassionately with those who differ. And living this way calls us to defend religious liberty for faith-based organizations and to advocate for antidiscrimination laws to protect people who identify as LGBT. It takes courage and civility to live life with a firm center and soft edges in a society that increasingly finds that "center" to be out of step with its norms.

When I became president of Biola University in 2007, I did not anticipate that sexual identity would emerge as one of *the* issues of my leadership. And I didn't see its rapidity. Some advised me to plug my ears and start declaring that we are a college that will not tolerate anyone who has gay attractions. We chose not to take that advice to clench our fists. Some advised me not to talk about it at all, to avoid being labeled as the antigay president at an antigay college, to keep my head below the radar and fit in with emerging norms. Conceding to cultural changes wasn't an option either. I hope and pray as Christians that when we face options like these, we do not settle on a biblically compromised middle ground. But I pray we take a higher ground.

Often the higher ground is finding common ground, the place where conversations take place. And we can look for common ground even when we cannot find a shared common good.

I hope and pray that an approach with a firm biblical center and soft relational edges continues as our way forward.

What does it mean as Christians to live the way of kindness on the LGBT issue? For one thing, it means we admit its complexity. Lately I've heard good people on both sides of the issue talk about certain aspects of human sexuality as "no-brainers." It's not that I think they're defining the space between their ears, but I do think they are underestimating the issue's complexity. Sexuality is not simple, nor is it constrained to simple labels or familiar clichés. It is, in fact, a "brainer" that demands wisdom, discretion, a lot of listening, and above all an increased commitment to a deeply understood biblical foundation for sexuality and for relationships. When God draws a direct parallel between the love of a man and a woman and Christ's love for the church, we know we are peering into a deep, deep pool.

If on this issue we listen merely as a chance to catch our breath before we ramble on, self-gratified in our own opinions, we are not living the way of kindness. If we listen hoping only to trap our "opponents" in a logical fallacy or a theological error, we are not living the way of kindness. If we listen without truly trying to respect the voices of others, we are not living the way of kindness. And if we are not living the way of kindness, then we will most likely forfeit opportunities for *our* voices to be heard, voices that give hope and point to the redeeming grace of a righteous God.

Listening is a dimension of loving.

The kindness of listening reveals our compassion. It

demands proximity. If we don't have proximity, we can't truly listen. If we don't listen, we'll have a hard time conveying with sincerity that we care.

Some perceive it to be a slippery slope when we listen to differing voices. I believe they're wrong, so long as our center is grounded. That is, so long as we hold to biblical orthodoxy and we long for others to see through us the redeeming and rescuing love of Christ. Earnest listening is *not* incompatible with earnest conviction. A life of radical kindness and a life of biblical faithfulness are not mutually exclusive. They are mutually dependent. It's a firm center and soft edges.

One thing I've noticed in my handful of years leading a university is that this generation is less interested in fighting their parents' "culture war" coercion battles and more interested in the art of relational persuasion. It's essential to have convictions, but leading conversations with convictions may be a less effective strategy than leading conversations with kindness. But we cannot do compassion without conviction.

At our university, where in recent years one of our catchphrases has been "think biblically about everything," we commissioned a team of faculty to draft a paper that addresses a scriptural ethic on human sexuality. The team did this by looking theologically and pastorally at the breadth of biblical texts rather than knitting together one side's proof texts while ignoring the other's. This thoughtful paper became a framework for our conversations, and it gave us the context to invite guests with differing perspectives to our community for respectful discussions.

By happenstance or providence, this long-in-the-making paper was released the day after signs and flyers and QR codes were surreptitiously posted around campus to announce the launch of Biola Queer Underground. BQU came out as an anonymous and unofficial group whose intent—as I understood it—was twofold. First, the group wanted to raise awareness about the existence of same-sex attracted Biola students and graduates. Second, the group wanted the university to change its policy on restricting how students with same-sex attractions behave. The media pounced. Local papers and national news services like MSNBC, Fox, and the *Huffington Post* picked up the story. Blogs lit up, revealing the obvious truth that social media, absent relationships, can be toxic, from every side.

Our heads had risen above the radar.

The university's communications team responded thoughtfully with press releases and statements. We had spokespersons give perspective to our position. I even gave a "family talk" chapel address to the student body, my first address on human sexuality. I believe these were the right responses, but I also began to understand the difference in leadership between problems we solve and challenges we live with and learn from. This was a challenge we needed to live with and learn from.

A few weeks after the Biola Queer Underground debut, I reached out to a few gay or questioning alumni. They were all in the Northeast, and as I would be visiting Boston soon, I asked if they would meet me over a meal just to talk. They quickly obliged. Two were psychologists and one was an Ivy League doctoral student.

For several hours I met with these three at the Depot Diner in North Beverly, Massachusetts, over hash browns and eggs. We agreed not to discuss theology. Instead, I wanted to hear about their experiences as students coming to terms with their own sexuality.

That morning, August 2, 2012, stands out as one of the most important listening moments of my career. Any uptightness on their part seemed to wane with each coffee refill. I listened as one of them reflected about the sense of futility on trying to reverse his same-sex attraction. I heard about the demeaning comments of classmates who would rather lob a thoughtless word than love a struggling peer. I heard of residence hall neighbors who came alongside them with compassion. I heard tender stories of faculty who listened and counseled, slow to judge and quick to linger in conversation. I heard of faculty who didn't.

As I paid the check and got back in my car, I felt a mixture of grief and gratitude. I grieved for the experiences of these graduates and our students with same-sex attraction who are treated as "less than" by other Christians. I continue to grieve even more broadly for followers of Jesus who make choices inconsistent with the truths of Scripture. At the same time, I was grateful for their honesty and for the dimensions of their stories of those in the Christian community who came alongside them, quick to listen and slow to challenge.

I listened and I learned that morning, hearing enough to

know that the candor of alumni like these needed an audience on campus. So that's what we did.

The attendance that afternoon several months later exceeded my expectations. Faculty members poured into the university's largest banquet room. Three alumni—including one from our Massachusetts breakfast—made their way to the panelists' chairs. The format was for the two men and one woman to unpack their Biola stories in the context of their journeys. There were tears and there were pleas. Those of us listening intently did so with great respect for the vulnerability of our guests as they recounted their wrestling with same-sex attraction and their journeys since. These three graduates of the university shook no fists and raised no voices. And the audience's questions were heartfelt, not bait. The sustained applause at the end bespoke the sincerity of the listeners.

Though the conversation did not change the university's interpretation of the biblical position—nor was it intended to do so—it did change some hearts to be inclined to listen more and categorize less.

Kindness that bends to accept as valid everyone else's viewpoint is not kindness. We can be kind *and* strong in our perspective. We can be kind *and* encourage one another toward purity before God. We can be kind *and* lovingly persuade someone to at least consider our perspective on what the Bible teaches. Kindness is not built thoughtlessly on the cliché that we "agree to disagree" and then never engage in conversation. Kindness frees us to hold deep moral convictions minus the vitriol.

Thoughtful Christians and biblically faithful organizations *should* make clear their position on what the Scriptures teach on human sexuality. This is one way our center is firmed.

And listening through honest conversations is one way our edges are softened and where our defenses dissolve. These conversations are rarely one-offs. They often have no finish line. They need to marinate over time. When conversations become friendships, all the better. Familiarity and proximity matter in conversations. These are tools for living the way of kindness. And kindness, Paul articulates compellingly in Romans 2, leads to repentance, to transformation.

Chapter 5

UNSUITABLY INTOLERANT:
THE WAY OF KINDNESS OFTEN TAKES TIME

*You have heard that it was said, "Love your neighbor
and hate your enemy." But I tell you, love your enemies
and pray for those who persecute you.*

—MATTHEW 5:43-44

What happens when we're the only one interested in having the conversation with those who disagree with us? Being kind sometimes means we're ignored or rebuffed, unwelcomed and left out to dry. That's the risk. Kindness should not expect kindness in return. A life of generous kindness doesn't mean it will always be welcomed kindness. Although the three alumni at the Depot Diner received me, I've also not been received, at least at first.

One prominent blogger named John Shore—an LGBT ally—wrote some things about me and a speech I gave on human sexuality that were harsh and difficult to read. Rather than posting a comment with arguments to outflank his,

I decided to reach out to John directly through e-mail. Part of our exchange, which I use here with his permission, went like this:

Barry to John, January 28: Dear John, If you're interested, in the next few months I'd like to have a private cup of coffee with you, just the two of us with no need for anything to be blogged. And no agenda. I know we disagree on some basic presuppositions, but I am open to share some time with you. You've written about Biola and me extensively back in May, but we have not met. May I invite you to a one-on-one conversation, brother to brother? Coffee (or lunch) is on me. Let me know if you're interested by e-mailing me at my personal address above. Yours, Barry Corey

John to Barry, January 28: Hi, Barry. I appreciate your too-kind overture. And yes, I would be pleased to meet with you—in private, as you say, and off the record. . . . I'm certainly happy to come to your office if that works for you. Thank you again for the gracious invitation.

John to Barry, February 5: It's nice of you to invite me up, especially given that in my piece about you I wasn't exactly Joe Generous. So your graciousness (assuming you haven't invited me up to shoot me or anything—which, as I say, I wouldn't exactly blame you for) is especially affecting.

Barry to John, February 6: Dear John . . . I'm really not a shooter. Yours, Barry Corey

John to Barry, February 20: Hi, Barry. Terribly sorry to bother you, but would you mind sharing with me why it is you'd like to meet with me? . . . Have no idea what you might have in mind for our get-together. Is it asking too much for you to maybe enlighten me on that just a bit? Thanks! Hope you're well.

Barry to John, February 20: Dear John, Thanks for asking. My invitation was meant merely to meet you and for you to hear from my perch about Biola's approach to all matters LGBTQ. I have no agenda to tell you anything or counterpoint any of your blogs. But I do think it would be helpful for you to hear about places like Biola and how thoughtfully we are responding to our students on issues of sexual identity. I just thought this would be a conversation in the spirit of Christian civility. That's all. Barry

John to Barry, February 20: Sometimes I hear from pastors or ministry leaders who are in the process of discerning where exactly they stand on the delicate

and so often troubling question of LGBTQ and
Christianity. It happens when they're moving toward
a change, one way or another. I'm not judging
you on this (nor presuming to think you'd care if I
was), but am I hearing correctly that your position,
be it personally or professionally, hasn't changed
from that which you expressed via the video of
the address of yours upon which I subsequently
(and so obnoxiously, I know) commented? Not
that it matters, really; it's just good sometimes to
know what to expect. But certainly I am genuinely
interested in how Christian colleges are rather
suddenly having to deal with this issue, and with this
unexpected nationwide flowering of student groups
akin to Queer Biola Underground. I don't envy you,
I'll say that. By which I only mean to show respect to
the depths of your challenges there. Not the easiest
row to hoe. And not going to get any easier, as
you know.

Barry to John, February 20: John, I still stand by
what I said [in chapel] last May. I also know some
of my words weren't understood as they were meant.
For instance, the "Pharisee" comment that seemed
to gather much ire was intended as equally pointed
at those in the anti-LGBT camp who use Scripture
to justify hate, bullying, disrespect, and scorn toward
their gay sisters and brothers. —B

John to Barry, March 11: Hi, Barry. I'm sorry, but I'm afraid I won't be able to make our meeting this week. The truth is that this weekend I received a few e-mails from family members of gay lifelong Christians who understood their sexual orientation to be at such odds with Christianity that they felt their only solution was suicide. I appreciate that you hold the views that you do on that particular matter—but I'm likewise confident that, at least for this week anyway, I will prove unsuitably intolerant of those views to be at all suitable company to you. I sincerely apologize for any inconvenience my cancellation causes you; I know how very busy you are, and appreciate the time with me that you offered. Best to you.

Several years later, I still haven't met with John.

I respect his self-awareness, acknowledging that if he were with me, he'd be "unsuitably intolerant" of my views. One day I hope to have that coffee across the table when John's more suitably tolerant of sitting down with someone whose beliefs differ from his. I think our conversation will be rich in substance and civility. I believe that day will come.

When John said he would be "unsuitably intolerant" of my perspective, I heard his resistance to tolerate what I might say given the heart-wrenching stories he hears about bullying linked to suicide. I read between John's lines that he believes the church can be cruel, and things would be a lot better if Christians would just change their views on homosexual practice.

Certainly we in the church need to listen to and love more those who are processing their sexual identity. Kindness never bullies. And we can do this without ceding our convictions of what we believe God calls holy in sexual relations. We need to give up some of our quick-to-judge critiques without giving up our deeply held convictions of what is wrong and what is right.

What does it mean to love your theological or ideological "enemy"? What does it mean to pray with sincerity for those who see things differently than you do? How do we fuse the verbs *love* and *pray* in Jesus' imperatives "love your enemies" and "pray for those who persecute you"? Sometimes we do one or the other, so that our love is prayerless or our prayer is loveless. Loving our enemies creates the way to build the bridge of relationship. It's the soft edge. Praying for our enemies is pleading with God for a transformation to happen. It's the firm center.

John's resistance to meet me underscores the years, even decades, of sharp barbs exchanged between sides. Sometimes Christians harangue but aren't careful to love and pray for those with whom they disagree. Sometimes Christians either love *or* pray, but not both. John reflects a culture that has become suspicious and distrustful of Christians.

Suspicion and distrust may or may not be erased over time through kindness. Though our *methods* of kindness may be rejected, our attempts don't need to be abandoned.

Kindness calls us to try and retry, to pray ceaselessly, hoping one day the moment will come for the conversation to begin that will lead toward hope, redemption, and new life in Christ. Kindness simply for the sake of being nice is profoundly unbiblical.

I'm still ready to pick up the conversation with John. And I want to learn more of what he means by "gay lifelong Christians who understood their sexual orientation to be at such odds with Christianity that they felt their only solution was suicide." Christians need to be in the conversation to figure out answers to self-destructive behaviors rather than just standing at arm's length and doing nothing. Christians need to stand against unrighteous discrimination of all sorts. I know I have something to learn from John on how Christians treat those with same-sex attraction—thus the invitation for coffee. And as John also responds in kindness, which I believe he will, he'll be open to listen to me on why I believe God is clear on how we live sexually. My hunch is his RSVP was deferred and not scratched.

In terms of reaching a world that does not believe God has a design for us to flourish in our lives and relationships, I pray Christians are afforded the freedom to express our beliefs with gentleness and respect. We should be able to do this civilly in the context of religious freedom and in a society that reveres pluralism rather than one voice being superior to another. We can do this as Christians, standing resolutely for what we believe while understanding that others have the same right to believe something different from us. This respect for what we believe is a two-way street, *from* Christians and *toward* Christians.

That means those who disagree with our understanding of a biblically orthodox view of human sexuality need to make room for us in the conversation and not outshout or close their ears to our voices. And it cuts both ways, as I've stated earlier. We need to make room to listen as well. But if in God's sovereignty the chasm grows and the pressure intensifies to cede our deeply held biblical values, may we not capitulate on Scripture but instead be willing to stand strong as an exiled people, pursuing as a remnant the way of righteousness as the only course, come what may. It won't be the first time the people of God have lived this way.

Washington University Law School professor John Inazu describes the life of a firm center and soft edges when he writes,

> We can choose to model kindness and charity across deep differences without sacrificing the claims upon which we stake our lives. That posture will affect how we talk to and treat others. The aspirations of tolerance, humility, and patience do not prevent us from expressing moral judgments or public claims of faith. But they will inform *how* we express such judgments and faith claims.[1]

We should not have to quiet our Christian convictions or muzzle God's voice to express our views freely. The heart of

America as a free society is that we uphold the right to beliefs that are different from our neighbors', and we do this best without hostility or acrimony. We do this best with discussion and civility. As president of a Christian university—founded and sustained on an abiding biblical worldview—I believe Christian higher education is an essential dimension of America's fabric, and our nation would be impoverished if we lost the heart of what we're doing. We care about character development that helps edges soften. We care about intellectual development that firms our centers through curiosity and thoughtful reflection. We care about having souls of conviction and voices of courage, courage that comes through an abiding faith in Christ.

For years I have kept a prayer journal beside my overstuffed leather chair in my home study. From that chair I write my prayers to express my heart more thoughtfully and to recollect later more accurately. One of my more recurring and anguished pleas before God is wisdom for how I should navigate my life and my vocational calling in the polemical issues of the day, none more contentious than human sexuality. The pages of the journal expose my petitions, my convictions, and my fears. Almost every day I think about this issue and try to watch the words I say, knowing the power words have both to hurt and to heal or to be misconstrued.

In my prayer journals, I have penned thoughts about how I can lean more into grace and truth. Some of my journal entries sound like this:

May a firm center of truth and soft edges of grace diminish the harsh rhetoric from those who speak without listening.

May this firm and soft posture not diminish Christians' call to speak forthrightly about what they believe.

May I build friendships and not walls, and in so doing move people closer to Jesus as love's truest source and most deserving object.

May I not abandon a careful understanding of Scripture as it was intended, even as it relates to sexuality. I must love deeply, as God's Word calls. And I must live righteously, as God's Word calls.

May an honest reading of the Word of God inform my opinions instead of my opinions informing how I read God's Word.

May I not look to the Bible to rationalize any of my biases but rather allow my biases to be formed by the Scriptures.

May I learn to stay historically committed to the Bible—as stated in the Westminster Confession—as the "rule of faith and life."

Truth is, as much as I am learning how to pray about this road, I don't always know how to hike it. I'm not always sure of what to say or not to say. My fear at times can quiet my voice. That fear does not come from the Lord. And so I pray that the Spirit of the living God will guide me and keep me strong. I pray that I exalt Christ in my words and actions and that I don't trample on the truth of God's Word in order to be liked or to join in cultural concessions. And I also pray that kindness—which means following the way of truth and being full of grace—will define me in these very difficult conversations.

On God's gift of sexual intimacy, I read Scripture saying clearly that his design is for this sacred physical union to be between a wife and a husband. I feel like I'd be doing contortions with the Bible's meaning to see this any other way. Yet it's also true that God's ideals for sex are *for* all of us and are broken *by* all of us. Unfaithfulness, adultery of the heart, sex addiction, lust of the flesh, lust of the eyes, and worship of our bodies are all entwined into our society's conscience and have become commonplace even among many of God's people. My sense of God's love as Father is that he has established a certain context for sex because he loves us and wants the best for his children, as any father would. Violating his ideal is happening left and right in a broken world and is happening among those on the left and those on the right and among everyone in between. I hope all of us, same-sex attracted and opposite-sex attracted, keep pressing for the higher mark of purity.

I am continually convicted about judging sin that may occur in same-sex relationships as worse than sin that may occur in opposite-sex relationships, the sins of the heart or of the eyes or of the body. We need to be serious about holy sexuality, that all of us strive in heart and hands to honor

God with our bodies. This is God's design, though all of us are prone to wander to imperfection and brokenness, irrespective of sexual bent.

A life of kindness in the conversation of all things LGBT means not touting marriage as the relationship we all should strive to enter. It's not. Jesus was single. Paul was single. We need to articulate a compelling vision of a new family in Christ.

The way of kindness means we never budge on Jesus. Our main challenge is often neither the political heat nor the viciousness of the media but faithfulness to Christ. Our challenge is that Christians sometimes wear a "What Would Jesus Do?" bracelet that reflects a life more informed by the culture they live in than the Bible they read. Scriptures are our foundation. We need to understand how God's Word was intended to be read rather than haphazardly reading it to prove our point as others are doing to prove theirs. Scriptures interpreted in their original context and understood in the fullness of a biblical theology need to continue informing Christians' understanding of sexuality, as well as of every other issue.

Christians need strong theological moorings in order to "be prepared to give . . . the reason for the hope that [we] have." And we do this, the apostle Peter reminds us, "with gentleness and respect" (1 Peter 3:15). We need to keep remembering that we don't beat an idea by beating a person.

Our identity in Christ calls us to live in Christian community, and that means we pursue affection in friendships with the breadth of God's people, not just friendships with people who look like we do. This means coming alongside our brothers and sisters who have same-sex attraction, welcoming each other first into conversations and often into life with us. With those who aren't married, we need to be careful not to herald marriage as the goal of every person and in so doing relegate the unmarried to secondary status. That's easy for me, the married man, to say.

I have thought about this more and more, coming to understand that life in community is far easier for me, with a family, than for those whose circumstances or choices mean they may live alone through much of life. Ignoring their loneliness is sin. It is a failure to carry their burdens with them. I've had conversations recently with someone who went through years of counseling to change her same-sex orientation without success. She shared with me that living this way is not without fears, explaining, "I want to have someone to call when my plane lands. I don't want to go through life with unwitnessed moments."

Her words to me were startling. *I don't want to go through life with unwitnessed moments.* For those who choose the road of singleness, or those for whom the road has been chosen for them, there is potential for genuine sadness when good things happen and no one is around to notice or nearby to tell. Kindness calls me to create community so that I *do* notice the precious moments of those who are single. Kindness calls me to create intimate friendships with them, friendships so deep that they call me when their planes land.

"I hope . . . homosexual Christians . . . take the risky step of opening up their lives to others in the body of Christ,"

Wesley Hill writes in the introduction to his book *Washed and Waiting*. "In so doing, they may find, as I have, by grace, that being known is spiritually healthier than remaining behind closed doors, that the light is better than the darkness."[2]

I hope all Christians also take the risky step of opening their lives to those with same-sex attractions in the body of Christ.

There is great dispute about how same-sex attracted followers of Jesus are to live out their lives sexually. I've noted my convictions, realizing many Christians will disagree with me—strongly. But for those brothers and sisters with same-sex attraction who have chosen to live celibately, may they remind me daily of the cross-bearing cost of discipleship. May I also consider what I give up as a follower of Jesus. I, who am happily married—what am *I* denying? I, who have loving children who meet me when I come home—what am *I* missing? I, who dream with my spouse how we might retire on our pension and live together 'til death us do part—what am *I* forgoing?

It's one thing to hold truth. It's another thing to come alongside those who are making remarkable sacrifices to live the way Scripture calls us to live. Practical ways of showing love are what the church needs to do more, not less.

Kindness means we are relentless followers of Christ, broken and in process. And kindness means we help each other become more like Jesus. We will have members of our Christian communities who have same-sex attractions and will live with these attractions for the rest of their lives. Kindness means we befriend them like family, we embrace them as made in the image of God, and we walk alongside them in ways consistent with the truth of the Holy Scriptures.

Kindness from our culture's point of view often means we must affirm the choices others make. But having soft edges doesn't mean we have to affirm someone's choices or beliefs to be kind. That's not biblical kindness. Biblical kindness means we love and receive others even though we may not affirm their decisions. We don't need to be identified first and foremost as being on different sides of an issue, as ideological rivals. This way looks a lot like an unhealthy posturing of power.

Instead, we need to be able to understand the true genius of biblical kindness is that our soft edges are permeable with another's soft edges. That means we allow our edges not to bump into others but to flow into others. Permeable edges make space in our lives for others to come in. We need to hold back on leading with a firm center. People will assume Christians have a hard center, but just imagine if we began to surprise them by our soft edges. When we don't flare up at someone else's differences at first blush, we allow others to open. So, let's lean more into soft, permeable edges.

We do well entering relationships when we accentuate our soft edges and not our firm centers. External flexibility does not have to equate to internal weakness. Relational generosity is harder when we differ on issues that deeply matter. But Jesus makes it a priority for us to love our neighbor, not agree with our neighbor. Jesus' incarnation was God's way of relationally demonstrating his love for us. "The Word became flesh and dwelt among us, and we have seen his glory, glory as of the only Son from the Father, full of grace and truth" (John 1:14, ESV). Jesus came full of truth and full of grace, not half of each or one but not the other. Grace is the soft edge to truth's firm center.

And soft edges mean we don't lead with judgment. Others are attracted to us more when we identify with their struggles. I need to let folks know that I'm in touch with my own sin, and I need to be careful that the log in my eye never comes across as less of a big deal than the speck or plank in anyone else's. "Here is a trustworthy saying that deserves full acceptance," Paul writes to his apprentice Timothy, "Christ Jesus came into the world to save sinners—of whom I am the worst" (1 Timothy 1:15).

May we be honest about our hang-ups and inconsistencies so that they don't deter us from the amazing blessings that come from following Jesus in the life of kindness. Jesus, the one who eats with disciples and sinners both and wins us with his love, calls us to do likewise. Let's not only be open for conversations to happen; let's *make* them happen. Then we'll see Jesus do his thing.

Paul writes, "Accept one another, then, just as Christ accepted you, in order to bring praise to God" (Romans 15:7). My prayer is this: *Father, you graciously accepted us just as we were, broken and incomplete. May we likewise be accepting of others no matter how unlike us they may be. May we be slow to shun and quick to welcome. May we lean into treating others with Christlike unconditional love and grace. May we have hearts that mirror your loving-kindness. Amen.*

Chapter 6

A SONG FOR THE BEREAVED: THE WAY OF KINDNESS IS THE POWER OF PRESENCE

Rejoice with those who rejoice; mourn with those who mourn.

—ROMANS 12:15

Dan is one of my closest friends, a Canadian with whom I've shared life as far back as I can remember. He's modeled for me what being an "all-in dad" looks like. When our children were in their early teens, I remember he referred to that well-worn parenting maxim "It's not the quantity of time but the quality of time" as false far more often than true. He dismissed this thoughtless expression as a lame excuse busy parents recite to shroud their guilt for not being present in the lives of their children.

Kindness often shows up in the simplicity of being present in life's ordinary *and* extraordinary moments. It's the virtue of being there in times of rejoicing, in difficulties, and in the mundane. The power of being there—of accompanying—means sacrificing our calendars and to-do lists to be all-in. All-in parents. All-in friends. All-in colleagues. Even all-in strangers.

For me, this does not come naturally. I always keep lists of tasks that have to get done, boxes I cannot check if I keep stopping my work to be present in someone else's life, especially when that person's journey is hard.

There's some irony in that one item on my list of New Year's resolutions was to have fewer to-do lists in the year ahead. That translates into being more engaged in each moment rather than always thinking of what's next. Even though I seem to falter, I keep resolving to live in the present, especially in my marriage and as a father. I have resolved over several of the past January firsts to scurry less on tasks and focus more on people.

I am naturally a scurrier, fidgety. I tend to pick up and shuffle papers, check e-mail, jot notes, fill the dog food bowl, wipe a counter, empty the trash, and pluck lint—all in the middle of a conversation with Paula or our children. Yet I recognize that these conversations are half baked when I'm busy tackling my tedious tasks.

Multitasking is the curse of presence.

When Jesus was touched by a bleeding woman in the very crowded scene of Mark 5, he wanted to know who had touched him. His disciples responded, "You see the people crowding against you . . . and yet you can ask, 'Who touched me?'" (verse 31). But the story says, "Jesus kept looking around to see who had done it" (verse 32). Jesus looked through the crowd to find the woman and engage her in conversation as if they were the only two people around. The disciples were too busy with Christ's revolutionary agenda to notice the woman who had suffered a great deal under the care of many doctors, spending every last cent only to get worse. But Jesus, incarnational and all-loving, gave her the gift of presence. He bypassed the crowds and spent time with this woman because of his loving-kindness. And then he called this nameless woman "daughter" (verse 34).

Presence is incarnational. It's the gift of being all-in with the person or people who need us most, undistracted by our lists of tasks and by the importance of our careers.

Early one morning I was going for a run in downtown Fullerton, the city where I live. Ahead of me on the sidewalk were two men. One was tall and the other not. The taller man wore jeans and a flannel shirt, his hair mussed and hanging well past his shoulders. The shorter man was carrying a McDonald's bag.

I decided to keep my head down as I ran by them, thinking these homeless-looking men might ask me for a handout. I didn't care to help them, and anyway, I carried no cash when I ran.

No sooner had I hurried past them, averting eye contact, when I heard the taller guy with the long hair say, "Hey, Barry." I turned around, looked up, and saw it was one of our university professors, a brilliant academic and award-winning author. I know our faculty salaries aren't handsome, but walking the streets looking adrift made no sense to me.

"What are you doing here at this time of day?" I asked the good professor, knowing he didn't even live in this city. He was aloof, but I pressed.

"Okay, here's the deal," he replied. "My friend and I every so often go to McDonald's early in the morning and buy a bag of Egg McMuffins. Then we walk around the city streets to find drifters, and we have breakfast with them."

I was speechless—and convicted. Here's a gifted scholar with a PhD from a leading research university who commands classrooms and publishes widely. Here's one of the important voices in his discipline nationally who was mentored by one of the great philosophers of our time. And he gets up early to have breakfast with the homeless. He's not just giving away Egg McMuffins. He's sharing a meal with the hungry and outcast, breakfasting with them. My first thought was *He doesn't have to do this.* My lasting thought has been *He's living incarnationally like Jesus.* In the anonymity of an early morning on the streets of a California city, this follower of Jesus demonstrated that the gift of presence is a gift of kindness. And it's most powerfully received when it's done while no one is watching.

One of the beautiful dimensions of kindness is presence. Being present with others when no one else notices is the kind of kindness God sees. It is the quiet gift of being there. Perhaps presence is the most profound act of kindness. Kindness led the professor to hold the world in his heart when no one else was around to witness what he did or to sing his praises. What I saw in this professor, who did not want me to catch him in the act of quiet mercy, is the virtuous way of living.

Kindness is coming alongside friends or even strangers to be present in their pain. It's one of the things Jesus had in mind in Matthew 10 when he said to his followers, "Whoever receives you receives me, and whoever receives me receives him who sent me" (verse 40, ESV). Being present in someone's deepest grief is one of the ways we make ourselves receivable, one of the ways we demonstrate kindness.

Quiet presence in the company of the bereft—providing neither answers nor hasty platitudes—is among the highest and humblest ways we live out Jesus' teaching on kindness. It's true even when we comfort the profoundly grief-stricken who are complete strangers.

I talked about this quiet presence with thirty-five Biola University Chorale students as we rode through the night's rain toward Jindo Island on a Monday in late April 2014.

The tip of South Korea's Jindo Island points toward the Yellow Sea. Since a few days before Easter that year, it also pointed toward the place twelve miles out where the Sewol ferry became the crypt of over three hundred bodies, most of them teenagers, most still wearing life jackets. They were entombed in the ferry's lower levels because the children obeyed the crew's orders to stay put as the massive ship listed, took on water, and sank. Forty-eight secondary school children were discovered in one room alone. By the time our bus arrived that damp and mournful night, over one hundred teenagers' bodies remained missing. Someone told me fifty-four of them were Christians.

Dr. Billy Kim, the person who had helped arrange our

tour and arguably Korea's senior Christian statesman, had an idea. Through his access to government leaders, our week-long trip through Korea was rerouted after he arranged the invitation for us to be present with these grieving families. We would visit Jindo Island. This was the restricted space where, away from the public eye, rescue workers planned and waiting families huddled. On Jindo Island were the mothers and fathers hoping their sons' and daughters' remains would be found so they could hold them once more before burying their children with dignity.

"We are only a short distance from what is today perhaps the world's epicenter of grief," I told the bus filled with solemn, formally attired chorale students. I heard one student across the aisle praying and weeping. I heard voices of intercession, some quiet and some pleading, as the bus pressed through the rain and along the winding road toward the camp of tents on Jindo Island. Another student began to sing, "When peace like a river attendeth my way, when sorrows like sea billows roll . . ." The three dozen other voices joined in their melodies and harmonies.

The police moved the wide barricade for the bus to pull into the controlled zone. As we gathered our umbrellas and raincoats, we knew we had entered a place of profound grief, incomprehensible to any of us. It was also a sanctuary. Reverence would be our posture. Out of respect, students took off their jewelry and left smartphones on their seats. We walked in silence down the half-mile puddled road. We passed a despairing woman, crying alone. The orange-vested officials on either side of us spoke in hushed tones. The South Korea Crime Scene Investigation truck was powered by humming generators. The tents we passed held families and rescue team coordinators and television crews and phone lines and cafeterias, perhaps even makeshift morgues.

We were Christians from a Southern California university, walking voiceless, single file through the night rain to a gathering of despairing Korean Christians. We shared no language and had no common friends. We shared only our humanity and a cross. As I walked near the front of the line, I thought about what it meant to be given the gift of mourning alongside those we did not know, whose heartache was beyond our comprehension. I knew this would be one of my life's great honors.

The tent was full, well lit, and filled with folks standing and sitting. Someone had tacked a Salvation Army banner across the canvas wall. We crowded under the canopy, joining the a cappella Korean mourners already singing a hymn of hope. The Biola students' formal dresses and tuxedos lent dignity to the moment. The victims' mothers and fathers and siblings who gathered were dressed in clothes they had likely worn for days. I looked at them in their rain ponchos and rubber boots, one with an FDNY baseball cap.

The chorale was introduced, though the chorale members kept their heads bowed. I prayed. It was a prayer with words from the psalm the chorale would sing, about fearing no evil when the valley of death is deep. It was a prayer for the fathers listening in despair, whose bodies were tired, who had wept bitterly. A prayer for the mothers waiting to hold the bodies of the children they bore a short fifteen or sixteen years ago. A prayer for the siblings whose lifelong pain was just beginning, pain most of us there could not understand.

We came, absent conversation, to offer our gift of presence and song. We had nothing else to give.

We did not come to offer answers, and I told the students so. We came to symbolize God's providence, that the months of planning for our travels to South Korea may simply have been to stand with them that cold and rainy night. Interspersed in my prayer, I petitioned, "Lord, have mercy. Christ, have mercy." The sound of waves, one after another, splashed against the seawall beside us.

Two months earlier, the chorale director had chosen the "23rd Psalm" as one of the choral arrangements the singers would learn. They had memorized it in Korean. Little did they know through their countless hours of practice that *that* song was intended for a rainy night on Jindo Island. With one motion, the director lifted and lowered her hands to prompt the first words. I stood twenty feet away from the vocalists and watched as they offered their gift of music as a gift from the Spirit. Music and Spirit commingled through the refrain of the psalm. With no accompaniment and at the pace of a dirge, the thirty-five students sang, "Even though I walk through the darkest valley, I will fear no evil, for you are with me."

After the psalm's "Alleluia, amen," four men stepped forward and slowly sang, in four parts, "Some glad morning when this life is o'er, I'll fly away."

The chorale finished their songs. The waves kept splashing on the seawall. The families still waited to receive their sunken children, the end of their mourning nowhere in sight.

A rural pastor shared a brief word of hope to the inconsolable moms and dads as they stared down or out toward nothing at all. Soft "amens" of the grief-stricken followed the preacher's words of spiritual connection. After more silence, the chorale broke the stillness with the doxology, praising God from whom all blessings flow.

A Korean television reporter stopped to interview us, and the head of the disaster coordination efforts came to express deep thanks for the gift of song and prayer.

Just as we had come to the tent, we began our silent walk back to the bus. I was among the last to arrive. The seats were almost full by then. No one spoke. I heard the same holy silence that accompanied our journey to the camp of despair. My comments were brief to these students, these benefactors of kindness.

Kindness sometimes shows up more powerfully in silence than it does in words. Kindness is sometimes seen in selfless acts of presence. Kindness works best when we identify with people's sufferings more than their victories, a thought I've pondered after reading Henri Nouwen's *The Wounded Healer*.

In his book, the contemplative priest helped me see that my woundedness is the door to ministering to others who are wounded. When we understand our own pain, we then become suffering ministers to serve others in their pain. Our own suffering is the starting point, not the impediment, of loving others through their suffering by our presence. We touch people deeply not because of our professional title but because of our personal openness. Living this way makes all of us ministers of healing.

When we are fully present in the lives of others, real transformation happens. Platitudes and unnecessary babble yield to eye contact and full engagement. The way of kindness does not multitask when someone needs us to zone in. Engagement cannot cohabit with checking messages on our smartphones.

Kindness shows itself in the power of the phrase "I don't know." It means refusing to nod our heads as we make up answers intended to impress. Rather, it means shaking our heads as we acknowledge that we may not know. Community is created when we are simply present, listening, looking deeply, and caring genuinely. The power of kindness is not in the artistry of our words as much as it is in the sincerity of our attention.

Presence shows up in many ways. It's forgoing a deal-making meeting to attend your daughter's ballet recital or to watch *Wheel of Fortune* with your shut-in neighbor. Presence is when you take gingerbread-house kits to a home for orphaned children at Christmastime and you stay long enough to help them make a sugary mess. Presence is resisting the urge to look at your watch as a lonely friend rambles, talking much but saying little. Presence is more eye contact than it is saying something profound. Presence happens when you give your spouse the gift of conversation when you would rather exercise the gift of lawn mowing. Of the many virtues my wife, Paula, has modeled for me, the kindness of presence to others is among the most noble.

Simple gestures of kindness are more often than not the stuff of everyday life: going for a walk with the widower across the street, laughing together as a family, sharing a meal with some long-lost friends, or holding the hand of the bereaved.

Presence is about deceleration, pressing the pause button, as hard as that may be. Presence more often than not is unseen and can be confused with being unproductive. Yet it is hardly that. Virtues are never unproductive. Presence is the virtue of patience, the neighbor of kindness in Paul's list of the fruit of the Spirit in Galatians 5. Let there be more patience and kindness.

Chapter 7

"BUT LEAH HAD WEAK EYES": THE WAY OF KINDNESS SEES BEAUTY IN ASHES

This time I will praise the LORD.

—GENESIS 29:35

I'm not sure I can distinguish between the way the Scriptures talk about kindness and the way they talk about love. The words seem interchangeable.

The apostle Paul rattles off a list of adjectives in 1 Corinthians 13's poetic definition of love. One of those adjectives is *kind* (verse 4). Love, the source of all virtues, shows up in the form of kindness. You want to know what God's love looks like? Take a look at the nature of his loving-kindness, especially to those who seem the least likely beneficiaries: the less fortunate, the immigrant, the lonely, the neglected, the abandoned, the friendless, the homeless, the jobless, the hopeless.

And the orphan. This is Gyeong Ju's story.

While in South Africa, I first heard Gyeong Ju share her odyssey. I was so moved, I offered her a full scholarship to the university, not sure whether I even had that authority. After several years and several conversations, Gyeong Ju finally enrolled.

Gyeong Ju is Biola University's first student from North Korea. She began her freshman year in the fall of 2014. Long before Sony Pictures was backtracking on releasing its controversial and ill-advised action comedy *The Interview* and long before an awkwardly coiffed Kim Jong-un succeeded his father Kim Jong-il as Supreme Leader of the Democratic People's Republic of Korea, Gyeong Ju was born in Pyongyang.

Gyeong Ju's father was an assistant to Kim Jong-il until the regime saw him as an outsider and began to intimidate him. Fearing for his family, he escaped to China with his wife and little daughter. While living in China, they were taken in by a Chinese family, Christians who showed them Christ's love. Not long after, Gyeong Ju's mother and father converted from atheism to Christianity, making the decision to follow Jesus.

Within months, Gyeong Ju's mother was diagnosed with leukemia and died pregnant with her second child, a son. Strengthened by the grace of God even in losing his wife and son, her father began planning his return to North Korea to share his newfound faith. Before he was able to return on his own, Chinese police arrested and deported him to Pyongyang, where he was sentenced to prison, leaving Gyeong Ju in China without her mother or her father.

Just as her father's faith had strengthened after his wife's death, his faith also strengthened through his captivity as one of Kim Jong-il's political prisoners. When he was released after three years of hard labor in a North Korean camp, he returned to his daughter in China. Their reunion was brief, as he felt compelled to share the love of Christ to those spiritually suffering in North Korea. He returned, once more without his young daughter. Once more, his zeal for Jesus attracted the attention of government leaders. Once more, he was sent to prison.

That was in 2006. Gyeong Ju has not heard from her father since. He was likely executed publicly on grounds of espionage and treason. This is often the punishment for talking about Jesus in the Democratic People's Republic of Korea.

While her father was in North Korea being persecuted for his faith, Gyeong Ju waited for him in China, afraid and alone. As she tells the story, late one night at the South Korean consulate in Beijing, God appeared to her in a dream and said, "Gyeong Ju, how much longer are you going to keep me waiting? Walk with me. Yes, you lost your earthly father, but I am your heavenly Father, and whatever has happened to you is because I love you."

The story is both wild and miraculous that led her—an orphan in China—to become a university student at Biola, but it is even more the story of God's kindness to the least.

"I know that he has called me to dedicate my life to bring

religious and socioeconomic freedom to the oppressed people of North Korea," she tells people today. One day she hopes to pick up where her father left off. "I believe God's heart cries out for the people of North Korea, and I want to bring the love of God to the people of my country who have had their rights taken away."

As I sit with Gyeong Ju and listen to her story, hearing the confidence in her voice that comes from the one who calls her "daughter," I am reminded again that if God sees such potential in the least likely, so must I. Living this way is a profound characteristic of kindness.

While leading a Bible study with a group of Boston men, I discovered a "least likely" story in Scripture that I'd read and reread but had never fully grasped.

For over a hundred and fifty years, Boston's Union Club—established to build support for the Northern cause during the Civil War—has been a gathering place for men, mostly, to talk about the issues of the day, politics and otherwise. I was part of the otherwise. For a few years before I left the East Coast, I led monthly a Bible study at the venerable Union Club on the east edge of the Boston Common. The Thursday morning gatherings drew eighty or so. It was an opportunity for the faithful and the curious to meet over breakfast. We talked around tables and listened to the Scriptures explained in real-life terms. The speakers rotated among a Congregationalist, an Episcopalian, a Catholic, and me, a seminary dean at an evangelical school of theology.

One Thursday each month it was my turn to talk. I stood

in the room where prominent Bostonians like Ralph Waldo Emerson and Oliver Wendell Holmes had debated and pontificated. I was unworthy company, to say the least. Over the course of my five years at the old wooden lectern, I talked through twenty-one chapters of Genesis, one month at a time. The Genesis narrative is chock-full of complex and chaotic stories. Stories of God's people on a journey—broken folks with messed-up lives who stumble on and stumble through crises, learning to lean into God's promises on the crooked road. I often found myself in those Genesis narratives. Most of us at the Union Club did.

As I rambled month by month through the chapters of Genesis, something in me was kindled by Leah's story. Hers is fundamentally a story about a kindness that sees others as God sees them, not how our culturally programmed eyes see them.

The day I told the story of this outcast woman to this highbrow room filled with Boston businessmen, it seemed an odd juxtaposition. The room of men, many of them husbands and fathers, was about to listen to a story that shed a warped light on some husbands and fathers in the Bible. It was quiet that day as I spoke about a girl who was shunned by both these important men in her life. This precious daughter never fully understood the love of a father until she saw the love of her Father.

On first read, Genesis 29 sounds like a love story. But when I read it carefully and shared it with these investment bankers and educators and high-tech administrators, I saw it as a story about the mission of God emerging out of a messy family situation. The chapter opens with Jacob—Abraham's grandson—fleeing from his family after big problems with his dad, Isaac; his mother, Rebekah; and his twin brother, Esau.

After being on the lam for many days, Jacob arrives at his grandfather's old hometown, a town he has never visited. The first place Jacob comes to is a well in a field where the townsfolk gather with their sheep.

As Jacob waits for someone to roll the stone off the mouth of the well, *she* shows up, a shepherdess. She is gorgeous, this stunning young woman named Rachel. Jacob is transfixed. Perhaps trying to impress her, he rolls that large stone off the well's opening. I reminded the breakfast eaters of the backdrop of the story. This was Jacob, who hung out in the pantry, not the gym like his brother Esau. Esau the hunter was more Russell Crowe. Jacob the chef was more Wolfgang Puck.

The men of the Union Club, many unfamiliar with this story, listened intently to the romantic intrigue that started the chapter. So far so good. Jacob is the unmarried son of a wealthy family. Rachel is the beautiful girl who catches his glance. I'm sure some of the Boston businessmen began to fast-forward in their imaginations to what would be the amorous outcome of the couple's encounter by the well.

His manly, stone-moving exploit works that day, and Jacob and Rachel begin to talk. Soon, Jacob discovers that Rachel is his kin. She runs to tell her dad, whose name is Laban—Jacob's uncle—and it becomes this big, happy family reunion. And Jacob and Rachel marry and live happily ever after.

Well, not really.

Laban also has an *older* daughter, Leah. The way Genesis describes Leah in comparison to Rachel is a bit awkward: "Leah had weak eyes, but Rachel had a lovely figure and was beautiful" (29:17).

It's not clear what "weak eyes" means. I don't think the problem was with Leah's vision, like she needed LASIK surgery. The Bible doesn't compare how accurately Leah read the eye chart to how Rachel did. The story says, "Leah had weak eyes, but Rachel had a lovely figure and was beautiful." Read: Rachel was dazzling, and her older sister wasn't.

In other words, whatever was wrong with Leah's eyes, it had something to do with her looks. The comparison is between Leah's weak eyes and Rachel's lovely form, her body. Something about Leah, especially in comparison to her younger sister, was unattractive.

I told the curious men at the Union Club—many of them fathers—that for her entire life, Leah had to live with her stunningly beautiful sister, Rachel. Rachel was the sister who transfixed men and caused them to roll large stones away for her. Men looked right past Leah and saw Rachel. Jacob was one of those men. I could have been too.

Enthralled by Rachel, Jacob says to Laban, "I'll work for you seven years in return for your younger daughter Rachel" (Genesis 29:18). So Jacob serves Laban seven years to get Rachel, and in a way that is borderline sappy, the story says the seven years "seemed like only a few days to him because of his love for her" (verse 20).

Finally, the long-awaited wedding day arrives. The pageantry begins, and Laban brings together all the people and holds this incredible feast. When the revelry ends, the honeymoon starts. Jacob enters the wedding chamber for the night he's been awaiting for seven years.

At this point in the story, no one in the Union Club dining room was checking his smartphone or getting up for another cup of New England Coffee Company joe. It's the wedding night, and married men in the room flashed back to what was while the unmarried flashed forward to what might be. Some listening had no idea stories of honeymoon chambers were included in the Holy Scriptures. I continued, revealing the unforeseen plot twist.

Laban, the new father-in-law, has a ruse in mind for Jacob, his new son-in-law. He'll sneak the weak-eyed Leah into the bridal chamber for the honeymoon night, instead of the eye-catching Rachel, hoping a tanked-up Jacob might not discover until morning. Then Leah by *consummation* will be Jacob's wife, not Rachel.

The story says, "But when evening came, he took his daughter Leah and gave her to Jacob, and Jacob lay with her. . . . When morning came, there was Leah" (Genesis 29:23, 25).

"When morning came, there was Leah." Six angering words for Jacob. Six painful words for Leah. Perhaps Jacob rolled over at daybreak, saw Leah, and yelled, "You?!"

Jacob flees the honeymoon chamber and tracks down Laban, and an argument breaks out between them, two of the closest men in Leah's life.

"What is this you have done to me?" Jacob demands.

"I served you for Rachel, didn't I? Why have you deceived me?" (Genesis 29:25).

Though we were a dining room full of men, I asked them to think about this story from Leah's perspective, what her keen ears heard and her weak eyes saw. Imagine the despair of the wedding night as maybe Jacob kept saying the name *Rachel* in the dark, thinking he was with Leah's more beautiful and younger sister. How might she have felt when Jacob awoke to discover the woman he was with was Leah, the weaker-eyed, older sister?

When morning came, there was Leah.

Laban, her father, didn't want her. Jacob, her new husband, didn't want her.

Perhaps Leah eavesdropped on the shouting match between these two men over this ugly trick, her self-esteem eroding as their tempers flared. To make matters worse, Laban gives Rachel in marriage to Jacob a week later.

Already living in her ravishing sister's shadow, she's rejected by her dad, who wants to give her away. He is in essence saying, "You'll never be noticed by a man." *Leah had weak eyes, but Rachel was beautiful.*

The husbands and fathers who climbed the old wooden stairs of the Union Club that morning began to feel this older daughter's pain. Laban doesn't see Leah as a princess or his precious little girl. Jacob doesn't see Leah as the bride of his youth, the woman of his dreams. So Leah—the desperate housewife—tries to win the love of Jacob, of Laban, of anyone.

I read to the men how the story describes Leah's longing to be loved by her husband:

> When the LORD saw that Leah was not loved, he enabled her to conceive, but Rachel remained childless. Leah became pregnant and gave birth to a son. She named him Reuben, for she said, "It is because the LORD has seen my misery. Surely my husband will love me now." She conceived again, and when she gave birth to a son she said, "Because the LORD heard that I am not loved, he gave me this one too." So she named him Simeon. Again she conceived, and when she gave birth to a son she said, "Now at last my husband will become attached to me, because I have borne him three sons." So he was named Levi. (Genesis 29:31-34)

The men that morning not only grasped the story of Leah, they seemed grasped by it. They got it that over the years, Leah saw Jacob—the man she longed for—fawning over her younger sister, and she wished *she* were the one he desired. Leah wanted to be loved and wanted these babies to prove to her husband and maybe to her father she *was* worth something. She *was* worth being loved and pursued. She *did* have a purpose. Deep inside her soul Leah desired for someone to see beyond her weak eyes and love her for who she was as a daughter of God, created in his image.

Then, I told the roomful of Thursday morning Bible

studiers, kindness showed up for Leah in the most beautiful way. Leah saw the kindness of God. Her eyes were opened, and she began to see that someone truly loved her. The story says she stopped yielding her heart to those who would not receive it, and instead she yielded her heart to God. And in this whole messy saga of her life, she began to see clearly who she was, her mission and purpose and calling. And it happened because she came to understand that God had been noticing her all along. The story says, "The LORD saw . . . Leah" (Genesis 29:31). But it took her a while to notice.

Leah had been letting people name her, label her, define her. She was letting other people determine her value. She needed to see her value as God saw it and to receive God's grace as *he* wanted her to receive it. Leah needed to love *herself* through *his* love.

Then comes another baby. She conceives again, and when she gives birth to a son, she says, "This time I will praise the LORD" (Genesis 29:35).

This time I will find my identity in the one who created me and loves me and knows me and has a purpose for my life. *This time* I will look up at my Redeemer with praise and not look down on myself in shame. *This time* I will be defined as a woman loved deeply by my Lord.

"So she named [her boy] Judah. Then she stopped having children" (Genesis 29:35).

Three times she turned to Jacob for the love and acceptance she craved. Each time, she came up empty. We feel the heartache. But this time she turned to the Lord. And perhaps this young mother's weak eyes began to well up as they opened up.

Read the story with Leah in mind, I told the men sitting at the tables in the dining room, and you'll understand that God sees beauty differently than we do. He sees beauty in a way Jacob didn't, Rachel didn't, Laban didn't, society doesn't, sometimes the church doesn't, and I don't. It's why we need to keep coming back to this story. It's a "God makes things beautiful" story far more than a "we've got a great marriage" story.

That last comment elicited nods from several men in the room.

When everyone else was seeing a problem or an inconvenience, God felt Leah's anguish and saw her beauty. And she began to bear children: Reuben, Simeon, Levi, Judah. And that fourth son, Judah, became the tribe that would bring about the royal line. King David would descend from the tribe of Judah. So would Solomon. So would a man named Joseph, who would be the earthly father of the Christ child, born in a manger.

Jesus came from Leah's seed. Leah—the unloved, the unattractive, the unwanted, the weak—would become the ancestor of Jesus? Go figure.

Out of the messiness and unsightly dimensions of life, beauty emerges, and Leah says, "This time I will praise the LORD and allow him to define me!" Though the rough road of this story continues in chapter 30 when she and her sister further manipulate things to win Jacob's favor, Leah is beginning to see grace amidst the self-doubt.

The way of kindness understands beauty this way. The way of kindness sees in others not what Jacob or Laban saw, but what God saw. Kindness from God's point of view sees the extraordinary in the ordinary. And the extraordinary then becomes part of God's redemptive work in a broken world.

The way of kindness refuses to believe when people say, "God doesn't need me. Not with my background. Not with my story. Not with my pain. Not from my family. Not someone who looks and feels like I do." As we live the way of kindness—seeing the beauty in others—we deter them from buying into the evil one's scheme that they are not good enough, smart enough, loved enough, lovely enough, outgoing enough, affirmed enough, righteous enough, rich enough, or assertive enough for God to do beautiful things through us.

I told the men that morning that if we believe that God could never use the lowest or the most ordinary to fulfill his purposes in this world, we should tear Genesis 29 out of our Bibles.

This time I will praise the Lord.

And after living to earn the affirmation of others in her life, Leah began to say, "There's only one whose affirmations I ultimately need. And his affirmations aren't earned. They're given to me by grace."

As the Union Club men began to toss their napkins on the tables and prepare to descend the creaky wooden stairs for another Thursday on the job, I reminded them that Leah's story is about God's redeeming grace through the messiness of ourselves, our families, and our relationships. What seems so ordinary or unbecoming in us, God makes beautiful and turns into a grand story of redemption.

God touches the plain girl with weak eyes, and he places her in the lineage of Jesus, carrying the redemptive line. And it is through Leah, not Rachel, that a Savior is born for the world. And *God* did this. When the Lord saw that Leah was not loved, *he* loved her.

Oh, and one more thing I shared that morning as an epilogue: Jacob *finally* got it.

In Genesis 49, twenty chapters later, Jacob on his deathbed gives his sons some instructions: "I am about to be gathered to my people. Bury me with my fathers. . . . There Abraham and his wife Sarah were buried, there Isaac and his wife Rebekah were buried, and there I buried Leah" (verses 29, 31). *Bury me next to Leah!*

God used an unwanted, unattractive, weak-eyed castaway to be part of his great plan of salvation.

I gave the benediction that morning, and the room quickly emptied. I think I talked longer than I was supposed to. But Leah's story was worth every bonus minute I took.

When I see life the way this story encourages us to, that everyone's got a part in living out the redemptive story of God's grace, kindness in me becomes blind to status or outward beauty. Paul gets at this in his second letter to Corinth thousands of years later. He writes, "[God's] grace is sufficient for you, for [his] power is made perfect in weakness" (12:9). Or perhaps, "His power is made perfect in weak eyes." Paul also writes in another letter that "we are God's workmanship, created in Christ Jesus to do good works, which God prepared in advance for us to do" (Ephesians 2:10).

God's power is made perfect in our weakness. Through his attribute of loving-kindness, God is preparing each of us as his workmanship to do good works.

By depraved default, I am more likely to notice the pedigree of others than the promise in others. I look for status far more than potential. The résumés that make their way to the top of the pile are not necessarily what should impress me most, though they usually are. Left to my own judgments, I quickly assess someone based on superficial criteria, thinking a person's too old, too young, too poor, too uneducated, too ordinary, too scarred, too scared, too broken, too sick, too lonely, too simple to be of much use to God as a voice of hope to the world.

Gyeong Ju is a reminder to me of how grace works, of the kindness of God to the least likely. Her story is not much different from the examples of the Bible. This is the spirit of kindness. Kindness does not allow us to sidestep those who are obscure or anonymous. Kindness means we see how God uses the weak-eyed and the orphan to be part of his great redemptive plan for the world.

The Scriptures are stuffed with examples where God calls the least likely—the outback shepherd, the prostitute, the unlearned fisherman, the despised tax collector, the hater of Christians—and empowers them with his authority to boldly stand up and stand out for him. And of course we can't ignore the scandalous story of the unwed teenage mother who gave birth to a son, laying him in a cow's feeding trough.

A kindhearted God takes the least impressive stories and weaves them into beautiful narratives of grace. The idea of God's kindness to the least likely struck me in Leah as I was working through the book of Genesis with those professionals in downtown Boston.

This is the perspective of the redeemed: we are *God*'s workmanship. Not society's workmanship. Not our spouse's workmanship. Not our mother's workmanship. Not our boyfriend's workmanship. Not our political party's workmanship. We are *God*'s workmanship, his beautiful creation, made in his image, created in Christ Jesus before even one chapter of our story was told.

The way of kindness calls me to a deeper way of seeing people, especially those who are "the other," the ones who do not fit into my "good, better, best" categories. The way of kindness calls me to see how God makes sense of the messy and unattractive to fulfill his redemptive work. The way of kindness calls me to do likewise. The way of kindness brings out the joy of others. That joy is sometimes buried under pain and insecurity and some dimension of ugliness.

Bob Masterson was our neighbor in Boston's North Shore before we moved to California. Before I left to take on this new job, Bob gave me a box containing a cross he had made by hand and tucked a note inside:

Barry, this cross is from my shop and part of a
project I have been doing over the last year—
designing wooden crosses from the wood that has

been discarded or unusable and bringing the beauty out of it, symbolic of our redemption. The wood that is used is cherry burl, from disease on a cherry tree, and spalted maple, from wood in the initial stages of decomposition. There are very few uses of this wood, but the beauty can be brought out by one who understands its worth and takes the time to bring out the beauty from what is worthless. . . . This is the inspiration behind the design of this cross.

Tree burl becomes a cross when the carver sees beauty in the decomposing wood. Weak-eyed Leah carries the seed of Christ because her Redeemer sees the beauty behind her weak eyes, and she yields her heart to him. Orphaned Gyeong Ju, when God reveals himself to her as Father, is called to bring justice and freedom to the people of North Korea. Throughout the pages of Scripture, God uses the foolish to shame the wise. God uses the weak to overcome the strong. God uses the things that are not to nullify the things that are. God, out of his infinite loving-kindness, uses that which has no obvious beauty to be of truest and most glorious beauty.

Chapter 8

THE RELIGIOUS MAN IN SEAT 29E: HYPOCRISY SPOILS THE WAY OF KINDNESS

*Dear friends, I urge you, as foreigners and exiles,
to abstain from sinful desires. . . . Live such good lives
among the pagans that, though they accuse you of doing
wrong, they may see your good deeds and glorify God.*

—I PETER 2:11-12

On a summer business trip to New York City I power walked down Broadway, connecting my hotel in the Upper West Side with lower Central Park, going from one appointment to the next. I had no time for detours. No time to browse the produce at Fairway Market. No time to buy a bagel at Zabar's. No time to look for an iPhone case at the Apple Store. My morning mission was uninterruptible.

Smack in my beeline and decelerating the morning's endless pedestrian stream stood a small gathering of enthusiasts handing out flyers. New Yorkers in the intense get-to-work parade ahead of me walked inconvenienced semicircles around those dispensing the leaflets, neither accepting their bulletins nor locking their eyes nor knowing their cause. I, the equally indifferent, was prepared to neither accept their bulletins nor lock their eyes nor know their cause. Then I saw one of their placards, something about Jesus the Messiah. Now what should I do?

A college-aged student stuck her arm in my path with an offer. "Can I give you this?"

I made a snap decision. I reached out and took a flyer.

"Thanks," I said with a brief smile and fleeting glance, grabbing the tract without breaking my stride. Five or six paces later, not quite out of earshot, I heard her high-pitched voice: "I go to Biola University!"

That was all I needed to hear. I quickly one-eightied and made my way back to the evangelists.

For the next few minutes we talked. For the next few days I sighed, relieved at my decision to receive her handout and, in a way, receive her. Like the flow of pedestrians before me, I considered walking briskly by, waving off her tract and avoiding her eyes. Luckily, or divinely, I said yes. And I was glad I did.

I don't know how many other times I've done the opposite, brushing people off by neither caring nor giving them the time of day. I don't know how many other times they've known who I was.

Many university presidents are better known than I am, far better. But this job comes with at least a certain loss of anonymity. Not that I'm famous. Hardly. It's more that some strangers may not be strangers. So I try to err on the side of smiling at those who catch my eye, grinning as if we've met before. After all, they may know me from a speech I gave or a university magazine page my mug adorned.

Once, in a hip LA coffee shop, I *knew* that the young man who said "hey" to me was one of our university students, and I gave him a hug. He was a stranger. He stiffened. Awkward.

The way of kindness, as a Spirit-born fruit, is the way we live and not just something we do on Sundays or holy occasions. As followers of Jesus, we need to consider that skeptics are scrutinizing us, watching to see whether our walk mimics our talk, as the platitude goes. The way of kindness means understanding we are being watched, whether or not we choose to acknowledge it. For those with recognizable faces, the mic is always on and the smartphone is always recording. If we claim to be children of God, many eyes are watching to welcome our sincerity or to scoff at our hypocrisy. They tend toward asking, "Aren't Christians just as hypocritical and judgmental as everyone else?" Sometimes, yes.

Jesus directs his ire most frequently at the hypocrites, knowing how much and how often they demean and cheapen the truth of God's character. When the people of God are more concerned with *their* image than *his*, Jesus calls it hypocrisy. The "woe to yous" of Matthew 23 become a recurring warning from the heart of Christ to those among the religious whose standards are disingenuous. Jesus scolds hypocrites: "Everything they do is done for people to see: They make their phylacteries wide and the tassels on their garments long; they love the place of honor at banquets and the most important seats in the synagogues; they love to be greeted with respect in the marketplaces" (verses 5-7).

I prefer to see my place card at the head table, not at the table in the back. I get an ego boost when I get a shout-out from the platform. So I'm guilty too.

Nothing invalidates the way of kindness more than the way of arrogance and hypocrisy. When our religious trappings do not sync with our actions, we've got a problem. After a flight from Chicago to New York City where I met an Orthodox Jew, I began to see this problem starkly in me.

My seat assignment, 29D, was on the aisle near the back of the plane. As I boarded, I noticed a handful of Orthodox Jewish men, distinctive by their clothes and beards. Just before the doors closed, one last passenger hurried aboard, bespectacled and disheveled. From the black suit, white shirt, fedora on his head, and tassels on his belt, the latecomer was obviously Jewish. He took the last open seat on the plane, the middle seat beside me. I turned my legs sideways so he could slide by.

The moment he sat down in 29E, he took out his cell phone to make a call. As he dialed, the flight attendant began her intercom drill. "Ladies and gentlemen, at this time we request that all mobile phones and electronic devices be turned off . . ."

As the voice rolled on, another flight attendant dutifully patrolled the aisle as part of her FAA checklist. Politely, she told my neighbor to turn off his phone, as by now we were pushing back from the gate.

He wasn't done.

A few minutes later she came by again, downgrading her politeness to borderline scolding, insisting he get off the phone. He quickly clicked off the screen but didn't hang up—a trick. She passed by. He kept talking, discreetly facing the window seat and hiding the phone behind his beard's bushiness and his fedora's rim.

As we taxied down the tarmac toward the runway, the flight attendant settled across the aisle from me in the jump seat by the galley, oblivious that my neighbor was still on his phone, now speaking in hushed tones. I felt a peculiar urge of justice to point out his indiscretion. So I did. Holding my pinky to my mouth and my thumb to my ear, I gestured to her that 29E was still on his phone.

At that moment, hell had no fury like a flight attendant disobeyed.

In a matter of seconds, she unclicked her shoulder straps, jumped up, and confronted my seatmate. He didn't see it coming.

"Sir, this is the third time I've told you to get off the phone! I will have the pilot return to the gate and the police escort you off the plane if you don't get off *now!*" Her voice must have hit 100 decibels, somewhere between raised and roaring.

Passengers from rows in front and behind whiplashed their necks to look. He frantically closed his flip phone and put it in his pocket, looking away and saying nothing. The in-flight rubberneckers went back to their reading or chatting. As the flight attendant left, my Hasidic neighbor glanced my way. I sheepishly shrugged as if to say, "Can you believe her? Bad luck for you."

Not long after we took off, my Jewish seatmate stood up. Squeezing by me once more, he crossed the aisle into the galley and opened the pouch he was carrying. I discerned it was public prayer time, though he was the only one praying among the smattering of Jewish men on American Airlines flight 358.

His routine was religious. He removed his fedora, revealing his yarmulke, and draped a prayer shawl over his shoulders. Taking the phylacteries from his case, he wrapped them first around his arm and then around his head. For the next ten minutes he prayed with all the earnestness of the devout. From my view across the aisle, he seemed to do everything just right, affixing the band to his left forearm and the Scriptures to his forehead, kissing the shawl and gently nodding. Throughout, this religious man lipped the words of prayers and blessings he'd learned as a child.

When he said his final amen, I tucked in my legs sideways once more so he could return to his seat. He straightaway began reading a Hebrew text, continuing his holy task. Seeing his actions on the phone and then in the galley, I was honestly flummoxed. A few times my lips began to form the words to ask him about what seemed like two starkly different ethics, but I inhaled them before they were spoken.

Not long before we landed, and shortly after he put away his text, I could hold my question no longer. "Excuse me, sir," I said, exhaling the words. "May I ask you something?"

He looked up.

"You know, I'm not religious like you are," I began somewhat truthfully. I am religious, but not like he is.

"I'm not judging or anything," I went on, trying to soften the defensiveness I anticipated might follow. "But I find it a bit interesting if not ironic how careful you were to obey all the rules when you prayed, but you didn't seem to care about the FAA rules the flight attendant was trying to enforce." As the words were coming out of my mouth, I wondered what had come over me. But the words kept rolling. "How do you reconcile obeying religious rules but not federal airline rules?"

His retort was quick and protective. "I turned off the phone as soon as she told me to turn off the phone." But it didn't happen that way, as I—along with the three rows before and behind us—could testify from the flight attendant's third and harshest warning.

He kept talking, and once his defenses relaxed, he told me about the 613 Levitical laws he attempts to follow.

"It must be hard to keep up with that many rules," I said.

He insisted it was possible.

Our conversation continued about law and freedom and what God had in mind with the laws. By now, he'd picked up that I was more religious than I had at first led him to believe. We kept talking until we separated in the LaGuardia terminal. He ceded little, and I blessed him as we split. He headed off to his neighborhood in Brooklyn. I took a cab to Manhattan to meet a friend for dinner.

John wanted to treat me to a steak at an upscale restaurant

by Pennsylvania Station, so we coordinated where and when to meet. We small talked before placing our rib-eye orders at Nick and Stef's Steakhouse, and I recounted to him my conversation on the plane. I told him about the phone and the flight attendant, the phylacteries and the Levitical laws. In my own spiritual superiority, I made a passing comment about the pretense of the religious man in seat 29E.

John, a thoughtful, Ivy League–educated financial executive, took the conversation deeper. He posed that as followers of Jesus, perhaps we are all prone to some form of hypocrisy, and what I witnessed in the Orthodox Jew was symptomatic of us as Christians. The thought had crossed my mind, but it was more gratifying thinking about the Jewish man's hypocrisy than pondering my own. The speck in 29E's eye seemed bigger than the log in mine.

Once our steaks were served and John and I paused to pray a blessing over our food—as publicly as the Jewish man had prayed in the plane's galley—our conversation intensified. For the rest of the entrée, our restaurant booth became a philosopher's table as I began to see myself, the occupant of seat 29D, as a religious man not unlike my neighbor in 29E. John and I talked about the similarities and not the differences between those of us who are—to one degree or another—obviously religious.

As I've thought about the religious man in seat 29E, the story is no longer about him. This story is not to stereotype the Orthodox Jew next to me. It's not to stigmatize devout Jews or Muslims or Orthodox Christians who employ rituals and symbols as part of their public prayer. As I sat there in the restaurant, cutting bite-size pieces off my steak, it occurred to me that we followers of Jesus are also being scrutinized more than ever by our increasingly skeptical culture. John pushed me to think about my in-flight confrontation with the Jewish man as more than a "gotcha." He pondered aloud whether the conversation between 29D and 29E wasn't a lesson on our own hypocrisy as Christians, not the Jewish man's. If so, then anything that smacks of hypocrisy will become a lethal barrier to living the way of true kindness.

The vice of hypocrisy is the evil one's tool for squeezing lifeless the virtue of kindness.

One of the first things I said to the pious man on the plane was, "I'm not religious like you are." But that's not completely true. I *am* a religious man. Maybe it's not obvious by what I wear, but it is by what I do. My phylacteries are the title I bear and the stage I stand on. My shawl is the Bible I carry and my license-plate frame. My yarmulke is the public blessing over the Manhattan restaurant meal. The more evident it is that I'm a Christian, the more others will scrutinize me to see if my life as a religious man—by which I mean a disciple of Jesus—is consistent, whether I'm doing "religious things" or "secular things." And if my Jesus is not real in what they see, they probably don't want to hear what we have to say about him. Hypocrisy spoils kindheartedness and authenticity, the very virtues that point people toward Christ.

More and more the nonreligious are resistant to the adjective *Christian* and unfamiliar with the noun *disciple*. More and more we are defined—right or wrong—by our compart-mentalized faith. More and more we need to be seen living as full—though broken—followers of Jesus. More and more we must accept that bearing the name "Jesus follower" puts us on display. More and more the skeptics of Christianity lump us into the "what we're against" types rather than the "what we're for" types.

Just as I watched the man with the fedora and shook my head at the inconsistencies of his behavior, so, too, are we Christians being watched. If we claim to be religious, we should expect to be scrutinized. If that man in seat 29E were some Joe Blow, I probably wouldn't have said anything about his dismissing the flight attendant. But because his appearance proclaimed him to be a man of the Torah, I watched carefully to see if his actions were consistent with the faith he proclaimed.

This is where my story is not unlike the Hasidic Jew's.

I posed to John while he took another sip of sparkling water that perhaps the double standard I saw in my in-flight neighbor is often my own problem too. Putting down his glass, he agreed. We discussed how it's far easier to hermeti-cally seal our imperfect lives in a holy casing than to expose our imperfect lives in a way that makes us look less "spiri-tual." My own quasi-legalistic upbringing was so concerned about appearance that it was hard to talk about how messed up I am. The Bible's admonition to "abstain from all appear-ance of evil" (1 Thessalonians 5:22, KJV) became my child-hood mandate, and that meant Christians were supposed to pursue at all costs the *appearance* of good—despite the fact that I am far from good.

As counterintuitive as it may sound, people feel more welcomed into our lives when we allow ourselves to open up with authenticity rather than appear buttoned up with our self-righteousness. Kindness can't survive in a culture of insincerity.

As followers of Jesus, authenticity always works, even if it's not always accepted. Authenticity is a main ingredient in the life of kindness. Our authenticity tells the world *not* that we're perfect but that we welcome others in their imperfections as they welcome us in ours. Authenticity reveals grace, and grace reveals Jesus. So when someone receives us because of our authenticity, we are living the way of kindness.

I thought out loud while my steak got cooler. What if the Jewish man in 29E had chosen to eat a little kosher crow when I confronted him? What if he had answered my question in a different way, saying, "Sorry. I should have gotten off the phone when she told me to. You're right. My bad. I was talking to my mother. I'll apologize to the flight attendant"?

Instead he exhibited no consistency between his religious actions and his decisions. It wasn't so much his mistake that threw me; it was that his spiritual aura became less attractive to me because of his lack of remorse.

Followers of Jesus are being observed more than ever by an increasingly polarized society, a skeptical media, a cynical entertainment industry, and a contrarian academy. Some of this is deserved. Some of this is grossly unfair. Still, when we cease to proclaim Christ in how we live, we profane Christ to those who watch. Maybe it's how we steward our money, hoarding rather than living generously. Maybe we drive through poverty-stricken neighborhoods on the way to our "vocational calling," oblivious to the plight of those who live nearby. Maybe we talk about racial reconciliation in biblical terms but don't care about building genuine relationships with those whose stories are different from ours. The gospel calls us to enter one another's stories, like Jesus, so that "in humility [you] value others above yourselves, not looking to your own interests but each of you to the interests of the others" (Philippians 2:3-4).

Maybe those who are spectators of Christianity see us as lacking kindheartedness because our deeds don't mirror our claims. To them, our values might seem out of touch, and we're too obsessed with "morality." They cut hypocrisy no slack. Mistakes and contrition, perhaps. Duplicity, no.

I don't want to convey an aura of arrogance and refuse genuine sorrow when I make mistakes. When Christians talk only about the success of their family and ministry and never unsheathe the reality of their sufferings and shortcomings, how can the watching public take them seriously? For the sake of the gospel, we should forsake the self-righteous way. To live the way of kindness is to be humble and incarnational. It's the Jesus way, walking among people in all their messiness and not isolating ourselves to preserve our self-imagined perfection.

By this time in our conversation over the long steak

dinner, John and I moved on to more mundane topics before ordering our crème brûlée. The evening that started with my recollections of the man on the plane had turned my thoughts away from him, the Jew, and toward me, the Gentile. John picked up the tab and we went our ways, he across the Hudson River and I a few blocks north to my Midtown hotel.

The lesson from American Airlines flight 358 has lingered. Today more than ever, our high and holy calling must be a low and humble calling. We need to increase our diligence to love generously as we live out our faith sincerely. We will do well to model winsome voices of conviction for the many who are watching us, whether from the church pews or the office cubicles or the campus yard or airline seat 29E. Otherwise, we communicate that our faith is a charade. The way of kindness is not cosmetic. It is from the soul. It's not performance. It's purpose. It's not mechanics. It's motive. It's not pretense. It's candor.

And when we mess up, which we inevitably will, defaulting to denial only pours kerosene on the flames of hypocrisy. People of piety must be seen acknowledging and owning our mistakes rather than spinning them away. We are name bearers, and the name we bear is Jesus. Whenever we separate our religious image from the rest of our life, we are living a double life, and this inhibits the way of kindness.

May we be known as people whose centers are firm, edges soft, faith consistent, and posture humble. We need to demonstrate humility in what we know *and* in what we don't know. This makes us attractive to others, and this is what kindness looks like. May we be willing to acknowledge our mistakes and not double down in defense. As a people of God grounded in biblical integration and steeped in a reasoned faith, anything that seems inconsistent is not only a bad witness but a betrayal of our claim that God's truth matters in all we do.

We must stay the course as people and communities, families and churches arcing toward grace and truth. More than ever, people are watching us. Do they smell in us the stench of hypocrisy? Or do they smell in us the aroma of Christ?

Chapter 9

THE FIDDLER AND THE GERMAN BOY IN WAITING ROOM A: THE WAY OF KINDNESS MENTORS

*The LORD your God is with you. . . . He will take great
delight in you; in his love he will no longer rebuke you,
but will rejoice over you with singing.*

—ZEPHANIAH 3:17

The way of kindness calls followers of Jesus to mentoring, joining others on the journey. Those we accompany are seldom the ones who will raise our social status or bump us up a vocational notch. They may offer us little but ultimately give us far more than we ever imagined. Mentoring is never a one-way relationship.

Ironically, while retreating for a few days to be alone, I captured an image of what it looks like to walk together in community. It happened the day I was escaping my familiar relationships for a retreat with Jesus in Canada.

Solitude restores me. When I took the Myers-Briggs personality inventory, I was given four letters as my diagnosis. I only remember the *I*. I'm an introvert. Introversion is not to be confused with shyness; I got over that when I was a teenager. But I've never gotten over the fact that I'm introverted. I enjoy being with people, and it seems I'm around them all the time. But my batteries are charged when I escape the ever-presence of people. Life-giving for me happens with my family or by myself rather than while working a crowd.

Every once in a while my cravings for solitary refuge— a soul Sabbath—hit the red zone. Paula usually notices first.

"I'm going to Spokane for some business next week," I mentioned to her before one of my trips. "Do you mind if I stay an extra day and come back Saturday?"

"Stay until Sunday."

Paula knows when I need the space to retreat. The team I work with at the university also knows. Each semester my assistant schedules a day here and a day there at the Sisters of St. Joseph for me to think, write, and pray. It's a quiet convent in the shadow of the Children's Hospital of Orange County. When I see "Sisters of St. Joseph" on my calendar, joy surges.

A few years ago I attended a symposium in British Columbia on spiritual formation, discussing it rather than practicing it. Truth is, I needed the practice way more than the discussion. When the symposium ended, my colleagues had a plane to catch to Los Angeles. But my plans were different. I had a ferry to catch because I had my breath to catch.

I was panting because of the stress and pace, the lack of margin, and the swelling challenges of leadership. I'd been feeling what my mentor called the burden of accumulated weights: budgeting, fund-raising, hiring, confronting, vision casting, traveling, schmoozing, speaking. Paula told me plainly and quite tenderly that it might be good for me to get away, on my own, for my soul to get some oxygen.

My weeks had been blending one into another with little reprieve, and I could hardly distinguish one day from the next. The season of "on the go" was so nonstop I kept my suitcase open in our bedroom because I was packing it again within days of unpacking. In some ways, my proclivity to push myself made me unaware the "productive" air was getting thinner and my slow, deep breaths were giving way to short, shallow gasps.

When life gets like this, I eventually see several symptoms. My pace is relentlessly revved and the burden of accumulated weight seems crushing. Some of the good things of life are pushed to the edges. I laugh less. Crankiness surges. My family attention is distracted. Sleep suffers. Workout routines get put off until tomorrow, again. I snack. And I am too distracted to linger in conversation with Paula, my children, or a friend.

And when my life's pressures mount, creativity gets marginalized. I lack the imagination and the spontaneity to write a fresh speech or to surprise Paula with a dinner out, no strings attached. I forget to remember to design a free day with my daughter, Ella. I watch our son Sam from the corner of my eye while I click away on my computer, too busy to get up and wrestle him to the floor. I don't pause to consider a quirky act of kindness.

Anne Lamott writes that when nothing new gets in, that's death. "When oxygen can't find a way in, you die. . . . New is life."[1]

During that particular season when I was trying to figure out how to handle the burden of accumulated weights, I decided to retreat to a quiet Canadian lodge. I was caught in the current of a vocational eddy. The space to generate newness just wasn't happening.

Knowing I would be at this conference in British Columbia and having a few days open on the other side, I reached out to a preacher friend in Vancouver who told me about a retreat center called Rivendell, which Tolkien fans know as a Middle-earth reference to the "deep valley of the cleft." That sounded good to me, refuging in a deep valley of the cleft rather than scurrying frenetically on the raw edge of the cliff. The good pastor Ken Shigematsu told me the center was a ferry ride from the coast and set atop a hill on Bowen, an island overlooking the Deep Bay Canadian waters.

I made the reservation for a small, unadorned room with a bed, a desk, a chair, a few lamps, and a window that opened. I had to have a window that opened. I needed the air to breathe, in my body and my soul.

I drove my rental car on the Trans-Canada Highway heading west for Horseshoe Bay to catch a ferry. Somehow I felt Jesus was waiting for me on Bowen Island, bad theology or not.

After parking the car, I bought my ticket and made my way to the ship. Grabbing a to-go chicken wrap and an iced tea, I followed the signs to Waiting Room A. The ferry would depart in twenty minutes, so I found a place to sit, quickly unwrapping the sandwich and beginning my lunch. I was still on the fast pace.

The waiting room was half full with tourists and commuters preparing to queue once the vessel arrived. Two kind-looking college-aged boys wearing shorts and T-shirts sat nearby, their legs propped on their stuffed backpacks doubling as ottomans. As I took another bite, I watched an older man approach the boys, a man I'd noticed in the ticket line. I surmised he was a musician, carrying two instrument cases, one larger and one smaller. He was dressed in black except for his bright sneakers and high-buttoned, clean white shirt underneath his coat. Having overheard the boys talking, this discerning seventyish man with a beard and hair as white as his shirt broke the ice. "What part of Germany are you from?"

The younger of the two looked up, surprised. "We are from Hamburg."

The man continued, "What are you doing here?"

"We're here in Canada for six months, traveling around your country."

The man continued probing, but I missed the next part of the conversation as an announcement told us how much time until we boarded the ferry. Reentering the eavesdropping, I overheard one of the boys ask the man, "Is that a guitar you're carrying?"

"It is. Why do you ask?"

"Would you mind if I tried playing it?" That got my attention.

The old man smiled. "You go right ahead," he said as he helped the German teenager open the hard-shell case. The boy situated the guitar, its body resting on his knee as he found his fingering on the fretboard. Then he began to strum chords and pick a simple melody on the old man's guitar. The teenage musician, from my untrained ears, seemed to be a beginner—good but basic. Remembering I was supposed to be in retreat mode, I leaned back and listened to the chords he played, waiting not for the ferry but for my spiritual getaway to begin. Little did I know, it was closer than I thought.

What happened next was nothing short of serendipity. As the teenager strummed, the man with the white hair opened his other case and pulled out his fiddle and bow. The German boy didn't see it coming, too fixated on finding the fingering for the chords on the borrowed guitar. The man sat down beside the boy in Waiting Room A, now filled with soon-to-be passengers, and asked him, "So, what songs do you know?" The guitarist shrugged his shoulders, saying in his German-accented English that he really didn't know any songs, just a few chords.

"Well, keep playing," the old man said.

As the boy kept playing—even through his mistakes—the man bounced his bow a few times on the fiddle's strings, listening carefully until he landed on the same key.

Once the man found it, beauty began.

This old fiddler and this teenage boy blended their strings into music. The white-haired man tucked the chin rest under his beard and began playing that harmonizing and improvising fiddle. The boy, still too young to shave every day, kept strumming the chords, increasingly animated and confident. Pure music came from two men two generations apart, oblivious to me and the others in Waiting Room A. The room filled with unexpected music from a master musician and his surprised apprentice. The man sold no CDs. The boy didn't prop open the guitar case to catch tossed Canadian loonies or toonies. To them, their only audience was each other.

The summer waiting room was now standing room only. The man and the boy kept playing. As they did, more than a few ferry-waiters stopped talking, gently nudging their traveling companions and pointing toward the boy and the man. I counted at least four among the delighted and curious who pulled out their cameras or smartphones to capture this makeshift duet, some recording conspicuously and others more discreetly. I was conspicuous. Passengers down the row craned their necks to see what they heard. Conversations quieted. A few tapped their feet or bobbed their heads to the rhythms of the man and the boy, two strangers to me and to each other.

Waiting Room A had unexpectedly become a concert hall as this aging Canadian and this German kid, separated by a half century and an Atlantic Ocean, played together side by side with common chords transforming into common bonds. They spoke different languages. But as that accomplished fiddler bowed his notes, the boy came to life, fingering those rudimentary triads with increasing self-assurance, casting glances at the man, who responded with nods of approval.

I wonder if that boy told the story of the fiddler when he returned home to Germany. It was one thing for the boy to play the man's guitar. It was something even more remarkable for the man to sit beside him and do what he did best, sharing his gifts with his unsuspecting pupil.

I called Paula from the top deck of the boat and recounted every detail of what I'd just seen and heard and how priceless that moment was, a musical offering as I began my Rivendell retreat. Then, as the ferry departed the Horseshoe Bay port, I pondered what had just happened with the fiddler and the German boy in Waiting Room A.

The image of the improvising fiddler deepening the sounds of that ordinary folk guitar lingered as I disembarked from the ferry on Bowen Island's Snug Cove three nautical miles later. As I thought about the Canadian man and the boy from Germany, I thought also about my work at the university and the dreamy-eyed students coming there for a new journey. I thought about how this rising generation arrives on campus with their gifts and their eagerness to experience a new place and to stretch their minds and hearts and relationships in new ways. They come with raw talent and enormous potential. They are the German boy.

Reflecting even more, I thought of how the way of kindness shows up in gracious encouragement. The older I am, the more I realize the need for old fiddlers to come alongside young guitarists as their accompanists, encouraging them with a sincere and selfless interest to develop their gifts.

I thought about the lesson from Waiting Room A as I

walked the few kilometers up the winding Village Drive to Rivendell Retreat Centre. I began and ended those days alone, wondering how I could be more like the aged fiddler, coming beside others to ask, "Where are you from?" and "Where are you going?" I questioned how often I was inviting myself into other people's journeys to be their accompanist as others had once accompanied me.

At each decade in my life, I have sensed a theme for the coming ten years. When I was turning twenty, I wanted to finish graduate school and live an adventure that I knew would be more difficult to pull off the longer I waited. During my twenties I had some wild and wonderful jobs, some that made career sense and others that didn't. I lived abroad for a year, finished my graduate degrees, and fell in love with a fellow adventurer.

My twenties were the decade of internship.

When I was turning thirty, I wanted to be mentored. I found a leader in my field who agreed to let me learn under his tutelage. I had nothing to give him and everything to gain. He was a man of profound experience in my field of interest committed to a hands-on investment in me, a commitment that continued throughout my thirties and beyond.

My thirties were the decade of apprenticeship.

When I turned forty, I was asked to become the academic dean at the seminary in Boston where I'd worked for ten years. From leading a small team of support staff and a handful of professionals, I was tapped to lead a much bigger team of professors and scholars. I stepped into this new role with no small degree of trepidation, and five years later I did the same with the presidency of a California university. The scale of change from the seminary to the university was basically a factor of five.

My forties were the decade of leadership.

At fifty, my most recent threshold, I have given thought to becoming more like the fiddler than the guitarist. What does it look like for me to take what I've learned over the years and begin to accompany others on their journeys? My desire is to locate my gratification not so much in the programs or the buildings I've helped establish, but in the people God has placed around me.

I want my fifties to be the decade of mentorship.

Who from a different background than mine can I accompany? How can I come alongside the rising generation just as those who were once my seniors came alongside me, opening my eyes to wisdom and truth, to theory and practice, to correction and counsel? Whom can I take to a higher place than he could have reached alone? The German boy never imagined when he walked into Waiting Room A how rich his music would become when the nameless maestro sat down beside him.

An older generation needs to seek out mentees. A younger generation needs to seek out mentors. Mentoring is a gracious act of kindness.

At this point in my life, I am more the accompanist than the upstart musician. I want to spread and not squander my life experiences—the failures *and* the successes—and pass them on to those God brings my way.

One of the most powerful acts of kindness is to accompany somebody on a leg of their journey, even when we don't see any immediate benefit. Truth is, what we receive will often be far greater than what we're giving.

In the past few years I've begun to see how effective it is to come alongside others with less experience. And I've done this by spending a weekend swapping my business suit and black dress shoes for hiking shorts and running shoes.

Six thousand plus students attend the university where I work. As I have come to know them—scholars, artists, musicians, athletes, leaders, writers, a rising generation of go-for-it zealots who are creative, hilarious, adventuresome, loving, compassionate, occasionally mischievous, and usually wise—I want to know them *more*. I love these students, mostly eighteen- to twenty-two-year-olds more interested in making a difference than in making a million. The energy they possess, the ideals they embody, the courage they muster, the convictions they bear, the affections they radiate—all of this is joy giving.

Each year, these students remain so young. Each year, I increasingly don't. I keep looking older as age does its thing. The university students keep looking the same, widening the wrinkle gap between them and me with each passing semester.

I needed to bridge this gap. So I had an idea not long into my new job.

What if I took nine freshman guys away for a rigorous retreat? What if we headed to Yosemite for three days? What if I chose a trail demanding enough to strain these eighteen-year-olds, let alone my aging self? What if we struggled up the open face of a Yosemite footpath with its one hundred plus switchbacks in the dry, hot August sun? What if we burdened our backs with thirty-five-pound packs, exacerbating the gravitational pull on the ascent? What if we did all of this no-pain-no-gain hiking so that we could encourage each other on the journey, so that we could bear each other's burdens? What if kindness showed up in hardship, stretching us? What if I took to heart rocker Nick Lowe's advice, "You've got to be cruel to be kind"—in the right measure, of course? What if this was one of the ways I'd mentor, giving back what has been given to me?

But over the years, this trip has been as much for me as it has been for them. How can I lead a school if I only know about higher education's economics or regulatory expectations or curricular structures? How can I truly be institutional if I'm not also incarnational?

The idea behind this trip to Yosemite is to go deep with a handful of students, stepping for a few days into their journeys and returning with the insights and inspiration to serve as an in-touch president rather than an out-of-touch bureaucrat. If I can get to know nine students each year by hiking Yosemite together, I figure I can know the twelve hundred other new undergraduate students.

The criteria for selection are simple. The university's admissions team provides me profiles of a wide range of incoming students who, first of all, demonstrated leadership experience in high school and, secondly, are fit enough to make the trek. We haven't always gotten that second one right. Outside of these two criteria, diversity defines these students.

Peter was raised by an intact family in one of the wealthiest zip codes on the East Coast. Another Peter was raised by a single mom and grandmother in South Central Los Angeles, where the streets rubbed against the values of his home, sometimes winning. Tristan's father ran a think tank for scholars and graduate students associated with Yale University. Marcus, a premed major, spent his high school years shuffling from family to family, rarely his own. Sometimes Marcus was homeless. Jose's parents fled Colombia, where they had had a successful life, to California, where Jose and his siblings struggled as the urban poor, unwelcomed immigrants.

Kevin golfed country clubs in St. Louis, the son of a tight-knit, Jesus-loving family. Daniel was born into a polygamous Mormon household, living there until his mother bolted with him and his brother and three sisters to make it on her own. Sam spent his first two years in a Bangalore orphanage fighting childhood diseases before being adopted by a family in Colorado. Now he's a biochemistry major wanting to give back as a physician, embodying the same compassion healthcare workers had for him as an orphan in India. Rollin was an NCAA DI baseball prospect living the dream, the son of a California state legislator and former mayor before his dad succumbed to brain cancer, rattling Rollin's world.

Over the years, I've hiked the same trail with dozens and dozens of students, all at the front end of their new journey. They have been from whole families and broken families. They have been African American and Asian and Hispanic, white kids and third-culture missionary kids. My simple desire was to walk alongside them for a few days at the outset of their university journey to understand better these students I'm so honored to serve. After that, each month I'd invite them to meet with me to process life, in a small way becoming their fiddler.

My first year of the Yosemite hike, I invited a childhood friend from Canada to join me. Dan, a rugged outdoorsman with little body fat, agreed and has led the trip with me every year since. Dan came not just to demonstrate for these students how to grit their way up the mountain or how to bust up logs for firewood. He came to demonstrate to these students the power of sustained friendships, my boyhood friend who has become my lifelong brother.

On Friday at noon we load the SUVs with gear and guys, beginning our seven-hour trip to Yosemite. The pattern varies little from year to year. A Starbucks stop in Bakersfield. Barbecue dinner at Todd's in Oakhurst. Overnight at an Anglican retreat center near the entrance of Yosemite, compliments of a Biola father and diocesan bishop. Saturday morning we rise early and head to Yosemite Village—showered and fed—to begin the toll-taking hike.

As we adjust each other's backpacks, making sure the weight is more on our hips than our shoulders, we're still strangers. The nine guys are trying to figure each other out. And they're trying to figure me out, their university president.

Through conversations they're looking for common talking points in music or pastimes or majors or families. Some don't stop talking. Some barely start.

The beauty of this mosaic of backgrounds begins to work in this new community as they begin to lean into one another's lives. A Kenyan cross-country runner tells about his high school to a film major from Chicago. Micah, who spent a few gap years after high school backpacking around the world, unpacks wild tales to Holton, a wide-eyed freshman who left the coziness of a farming town in Kansas, a town smaller in population than the university he now attends.

The nervousness of these nine freshmen about a road trip with strangers starts to ease.

After the first miles of hiking along a paved road we reach the trailhead, where we spray each other with Deep Woods Off! to keep gnats from burrowing into our noses and ears. While we huddle on the Yosemite trail by a shrine of rock cairns, I continue the journey motif I've been sharing with them.

Someone recently told me Christians need to stop using the journey motif. They said it's old, trite, and meaningless. I disagree.

Life is a journey from place to place, from season to season, from valley to mountaintop to valley again. The author of Hebrews describes us on the journey as wanderers, sojourners, aliens, and travelers on the way. That same writer says Abraham "lived in tents, as did Isaac and Jacob" (11:9). Life is in tents. Each year I metaphorically but intentionally

explain the "in tents" journey to the nine university freshmen. I tell them we will be doing life together for a few
days. And life together means hearing each other's stories.
I've learned that living a life of kindness means forgoing my
preoccupation with my occupation and instead entering into
the narratives of nine freshmen.

"Journeys are about leaving the familiar and heading into
the unknown, and this is true whether you're one of our students from Compton or Cupertino or Cleveland," I tell the
eager hikers before we hit the switchbacks. "Abraham, Isaac,
Jacob, and their families each grappled at some point with
moving on to a new place. When God called them to go, they
pulled up the stakes of their tents and pitched them in a new
place. So I've got this idea that life is in tents."

Each year I repeat this line at the trailhead to the handful
of outfitted freshmen looking at me, hearing what I am saying but not fully grasping the journey motif.

Each time I say to the hikers that "life is in tents," they
strain a charitable smile in response, not necessarily impressed
but kind enough to nod at my play on words.

Despite the hikers not fully understanding what I'm saying, the point is true, and I drill into it. "Each time you as
followers of God move to a new place and pitch your tent,
you don't know what's next. You'll experience those days you
want to go back, afraid of the road before you."

After the journey talk and some Gold Bond, we begin the
hike. The first long stretch is walked in pure silence. I ask
the hikers to ponder what it means to be on a new journey

in a new place with a new community. I ask them to reflect on how they want to live in a way that looks like Jesus. Fifty meters separate each of us from the other before we ascend the switchbacks. We walk that long, flat trail quietly while pondering all that is new, with all of our hopes and fears.

The trail takes a sharp left turn in the woods, at which point the grade steepens and the cone of silence is lifted. Before long, shade gives way to direct sun, and the rigor escalates as we begin the unrelenting stone-stepped path. Grueling starts at the Snow Creek switchbacks, a relentless slope with no relief until the natural water hole near the mountain's rim hours later.

After a pitiless eternity of hauling ourselves against gravity, we stop under incense cedar trees for some shade, water from our Nalgenes, protein bars, and apples. At that point we begin to tell our stories, one at a time, and over the next twenty-four hours, we keep the stories going. I invite the hikers to unpack their lives, the switchbacks they've endured, and the mountains they want to scale. They hold back little, and I am moved by their candor and idealism. After each pilgrim's narrative, the storyteller's peers ask three probing questions. We don't do anything else until the three questions are answered.

Inviting others to tell their story and caring enough to engage in that story is one of the powerful dimensions of kindness. When we care about our own stories or some hero's story more than we do about the ordinary stories of those around us, we miss an opportunity. Everyone's ordinary is extraordinary if we give them a chance to tell about their journey. We honor each other by caring about the unique journey each of us has navigated.

I think to myself as these students' odysseys unfold, *I never would have been this open to my college president.* But that was when college presidents wouldn't have taken their students hiking, either.

Day one of the hike ends on a rock overlooking the Yosemite Valley and eye level with Half Dome on the other side. The view prompts gasps. The awaiting watering hole catches the bodies of hikers-turned-plungers as they jump the fifteen or twenty feet into a bone-chilling splash, celebrating the end of the switchbacks and washing the accumulated coats of dust from their bodies. I jump too.

By the next morning, as the sun breaks the mountains in radiant glory, eclipsing even images captured by Ansel Adams, most stories have been told except for mine. We've eaten the just-add-boiling-water breakfasts, and the embers on the fire still smolder. Now it's my turn. To the degree appropriate, I'm transparent as I acknowledge my milestones, deficiencies, and setbacks.

The students ask me their questions. "What is it like to be a university president *and* a loving dad?" "Why do you take us here, and what are we teaching you?" "How do you cultivate your own walk with Jesus over the long haul?" "What keeps you awake at night?" "Do you and Paula ever fight?" "Does sex keep getting better after years of marriage?" Given their unfiltered questions, I keep my answers honest, leaning more toward opaqueness than complete transparency, letting enough light through without exposing everything.

As I am learning to walk with these students, I am indebted to those who out of kindness chose to walk alongside me in the journey when I had so little to give in return. They paid it forward, and I'd be a squanderer if I didn't do the same.

Before we make the descent, we go back into solitude for one more hour, reflecting on all that has happened in us *and* with each other since the SUVs left the campus on Friday. As they recount the past few days—the pains and the gains—I instruct them each to find twelve stones and to place them in piles on a high rock overlooking what seems like eternity.

When we gather again sixty minutes later, I come back to Genesis and the people of God called to a journey. I remind them that life is in tents, that we pitch our tents for a season and then we pull up our stakes and plant those tents in a new place. Where we are is the place God has for us, whether we planned it or not. And wherever we pitch our tents, there we also build altars. It was what Abraham, Isaac, and Jacob did when they camped in a new place:

- Abraham "pitched his tent [near] Bethel. . . . There he built an altar to the LORD." (Genesis 12:8)
- Abraham "moved his tent and came and settled by the oaks of Mamre . . . and there he built an altar to the LORD." (Genesis 13:18, ESV)

- "Isaac built an altar there and called on the name of the LORD. There he pitched his tent." (Genesis 26:25)
- "[Jacob] pitched his tent. There he set up an altar and called it El Elohe Israel." (Genesis 33:19-20)

Building an altar where we're pitching—this is our responsibility.

As the hundred plus stones are engineered that final Sunday morning into an altar, I ask these nine sojourners to consider the stones they're using to build their altars where God is calling them to pitch their tents. Stones of prayer. Stones of service. Stones of selfless living. Stones of repentance. Stones of self-sacrifice. Stones of community. Stones of Scripture. Stones of kindness.

One of my life's mentors looks back at those he has chosen to accompany along the journey and uses Paul's words from Philippians 4:1: "my brothers and sisters, you whom I love and long for, my joy and crown." Our mentor calls us his "joy" and his "crown."

As I look back one day at those walking the journey with me, long after I'm unable to hike those switchbacks, I have a feeling that there will be those fellow climbers I will call "my joy and crown," seeing that in some way my investment in them—pilgrims on the journey—has made a difference for the good.

I could not get the fiddler out of my mind during those retreating days I spent on Bowen Island. And I think of the fiddler as I hike the switchbacks with these eighteen-year-olds, talking life as we march up the trail. So much of the fiddler is in all of us, and coming alongside is a gift of kindness to those who look to us—with all our failures and successes—as mentors.

And maybe God was saying something else to me when I stared at the fiddler and the German boy in Waiting Room A. Maybe in some ways I am still that boy. And maybe for me, God is that fiddler—the fiddler who walked up to the boys, asked where they were from and where they were going, and then took the boy's song to a much more glorious place.

Like that fiddler, God is the one who graciously leans forward to know me and my journey. The one who welcomes my desire to do what I can with the gifts given me. And the one who touchingly surrounds my simple gifts and even my dreadful mistakes with his divine presence, transforming my small and damaged contribution into something of unimaginable beauty—indeed, a hymn of praise. As I pondered that fiddler making a symphony of the German boy's basic chords, I thought about the prophet Zephaniah, who said to God's people,

> Do not let your hands hang limp.
> The LORD your God is with you, the Mighty
>   Warrior who saves.
> He will take great delight in you;
> in his love he will no longer rebuke you,
> but will rejoice over you with singing.
>   (Zephaniah 3:16-17)

Over me? Whose hands too often hang limp? God will rejoice over *me*—with *singing*? Imagine that! The Creator and Redeemer is also the Singer, who sings over me, and as he does, he transforms my simple tune into his opus. That is what I also discovered at the front end of a time alone with God on Bowen Island.

Ultimately, our mentoring is not merely to help others manage their personal finances or navigate their careers or flourish in their relationships. True and ultimate kindness means we come alongside others to point them to the one who knows their song, in the widest and deepest sense of the word. My prayer is that over the course of my life I will be more of the fiddler to others just as God rejoices over me with his singing.

Chapter 10

NEHEMIAH AND THE BANQUET: THE WAY OF KINDNESS COMES WITH A HOT MEAL

*A hundred and fifty Jews and officials ate at my table,
as well as those who came to us from the surrounding
nations. Each day one ox, six choice sheep and some
poultry were prepared for me, and every ten days an
abundant supply of wine of all kinds.*

—NEHEMIAH 5:17-18

Enemies and strangers, the anxious and the suffering—
they can all experience our kindness around a supper table.
Kindness naturally shows up over a gracious meal.

Just look what David did.

David, the second king of Israel, endured a conflicted
relationship with Saul, the first king of Israel. To say there
was tension between them would be an understatement.
Saul's jealousy, insecurity, and thirst for power created a wall
between him and David, the shepherd boy who arose out of
nowhere to be anointed king. Theirs is a case study of leadership's darker side, exposing Saul's discord and dirty politics,
ethical breaches and power plays. The paranoid king was

passive aggressive, flattering David one moment and hurling a spear at him the next. Despite all of this intrigue, when David became king, he chose not to slander the name of Saul. And he chose not to turn his back on Saul's son Jonathan, the family heir of the throne and beloved friend of David.

After Saul and Jonathan died—from suicide and on the battlefield, respectively—it was David's moment to sweep the kingdom clean of any residue from the reign of King Saul. Instead of vengefully getting even, David chose the way of kindness, asking, "Is there anyone still left of the house of Saul to whom I can show kindness for Jonathan's sake?" (2 Samuel 9:1).

The only descendant David's servants could find was a boy named Mephibosheth, the son of Jonathan. He was lame in both feet. The servants of David tracked him down and brought him into the presence of the king. In the way I've imagined it, the scene is deeply moving. The frightened, disabled boy comes before the king, and this is what the boy hears from David: "Don't be afraid, for I will surely show you kindness for the sake of your father Jonathan. I will restore to you all the land that belonged to your grandfather Saul, and you will always eat at my table" (2 Samuel 9:7).

Mephibosheth bows and says, "What is your servant, that you should notice a dead dog like me?" (2 Samuel 9:8).

David answers the boy's question with a meal, and the Scriptures say that "Mephibosheth ate at David's table like one of the king's sons" (2 Samuel 9:11).

Kindness looked like a meal, the gracious gesture when

David opened his table to the least expected. The kind king invited the boy with palsied legs to sit at the royal table for every meal, every day. As the boy grew older and had his own family, the meals didn't stop. Fast-forward to the end of the story. We read that "Mephibosheth lived in Jerusalem, because he always ate at the king's table; he was lame in both feet" (2 Samuel 9:13).

Maybe there is no story of kindness in the Old Testament more poignant than the story of David and Mephibosheth. The contrast is not unintentional. David spread the palace table for the fatherless boy who was lame in both feet.

Kindness so often looks a lot like supper.

Food is what we have in common with the more than seven billion people around the world. Some eat too much, others not nearly enough. Food is the centerpiece of most gatherings and celebrations. My mother's kitchen was her canvas, as she created from scratch masterpieces of hand-made Swedish meatballs, homemade bread, and raspberry pie. Culinary art is among the few works of human artistry that vanish within hours of their creation.

At our supper table when I was a boy, we'd have guests whose names I can't recall but whose stories I can't forget. The meals at our home were often gatherings of strangers: missionaries and itinerant evangelists and church planters. My mother's kind meals warmed the conversations, especially among the guests who were the "every tongue and tribe and nation" sort. Sometimes "every tongue" meant I didn't even understand much of what they were saying, but we opened the table anyway. Long after my mother is gone, she will be remembered for her kindness that showed up in cinnamon buns and baked macaroni. And that is a worthy tribute.

Meals are often the starting point of kindness.

Paula and I spent seven years serving at a small Greek church just outside of Boston. It was a weekend gig where I pastored the English-speaking, second-generation parishioners. These were people with last names like Hatzieleftheriades and Orfanidis and Deligiannides and Kounadis. Once a month after church came the banquet. The grandmothers and mothers and aunties, gloved in hot pads, carted their best Greek dishes into the church. The small fellowship hall, illuminated by fluorescent lights, its aisles of folding tables lined with metal chairs, morphed into an epic Mediterranean feast. What was ordinary for these immigrant families was extraordinary for Paula and me: the spanakopita and moussaka, the feta and the souvlaki, the grilled lamb and the kalamata olives and the tzatziki, all piled high on my plate as if it were a platter. Over the meal old men told stories of the homeland, grandmas scooped out helping upon helping, church children taught our children questionable Greek phrases, and then we went back for more. Pastitsio and pita and baklava (and Tums).

The Greeks, from their generosity and out of their love, taught us a lot about hospitality. It's no wonder that when Paul talks about leaders in the church, hospitality is among the highest virtues. He rattles off in a letter to Timothy a litany of virtues, saying the elders need to be temperate, self-controlled, respectable, able to teach, and hospitable (see 1 Timothy 3:2).

For this modern Greek church, as well as for the early Greek church, the kindness of hospitality showed up in the form of a meal. It was never the grandeur of the hospitality but always the heart of the hospitality. Hospitality is the act of opening what we have—as much or as little—and sharing it with someone else. This is kindness. Kindness is often served through a meal.

Paula and I were invited to dinner by two young graduates of the university. They lived in the Echo Park section of Los Angeles, a transitional neighborhood—part artsy, part working class, part tough. So one July this kind couple, still newlyweds and still in their early twenties, hosted us in their apartment as we ate, talked, and watched the setting sun cast its long shadows on the skyline of LA.

Erin, bright and energetic, was hired after graduation as a nurse at UCLA's Ronald Reagan Medical Center. Jeremy came from Minnesota to Biola, turning down Stanford and majoring in philosophy. After graduation he was selected into the competitive Teach For America program.

These two young, thoughtful graduates asked Paula and me questions about life and choices, balance and family. The time passed quickly. We answered the best we could between helpings of panfried salmon, grilled asparagus, refilled glasses of homemade lemonade, and a sweet summer salad with fresh oranges and crunchy nuts.

We said yes to their invitation because they were kind

enough to invite us into their home. As we left their table a few hours later, we climbed the chipped cement steps up the steep grade between city apartments and got in our car to drive home, full and fulfilled. Their apartment was small. The chairs didn't match. The glasses were mason jars. The decor was simple. The hospitality was extravagant.

Meals put people at ease and lower anxieties. As they said good-bye at the end of a supper at our home, a group of international students told Paula and me that hosting them for a meal was among the highest forms of hospitality. I've been welcomed for meals around the world by families of modest means, who could not afford to take me to a restaurant, but they were honored to host me in their homes. I was even more honored to be invited.

For a few days in the homestretch of finishing this book's manuscript, I escaped the frenetic pace of the Southern California office for Windsor, Colorado, where precious friends Dick and Ruth Foth hosted me as I wrote for long hours at a stretch. Waiting for me each day was a meal, a gift of grace at a well-set table accompanied by wandering conversations. Kindness often shows up—as it did for me in Colorado—in the form of homemade soup and pancakes made without a mix (although it can show up in Campbell's soup and Bisquick pancakes, too).

Before supper on my last night in their home, Dick began talking about Revelation 3:20 as a reference to a meal. This is the oft-quoted verse captured in paintings with Jesus knocking on a door, perhaps the most well known by artist Warner

Sallman. "Behold, I stand at the door and knock. If anyone hears my voice and opens the door . . ." (ESV). My host during our supper together reflected on how the end of that verse often fades to nothing as it's being quoted. But the end is the best part. Jesus wraps up that knocking-on-the-door sentence by saying, "I'll come right in and sit down to supper with you" (MSG).

Jesus suppers with us.

Supper is as much the verb as it is the noun. Meals in biblical times symbolized kinship and acceptance. Jesus seems to be saying that if you invite him "to supper" with you for a meal, he'll invite you "to supper" with him for eternity. "Because when I was hungry and you gave me something to eat," Jesus told his followers in another reference to a meal, "you get the kingdom prepared for you since the creation of the world" (see Matthew 25:34-35).

Kindness in the form of reconciliation happens around the table. Grace is said because grace happens there. When Scripture talks about food, it's talking about our house. Hospitality is inviting someone into our space where life happens, and it's intimate and healing. Opening our table to those who wouldn't typically be invited is among the most radical acts of kindness. "Do not forget to show hospitality to strangers," exhorts the writer of Hebrews, "for by so doing some people have shown hospitality to angels without knowing it" (13:2).

Hospitality is a Christian imperative, not an option. Hospitality is the fruit of kindness, just as kindness is the fruit of the Spirit.

The cross is the most shocking symbol of kindness, the place where the kindest act in human history occurred. We often think of the cross as cruel and rugged and bloody and dark. But the cross is ultimately and eternally kind in that it is the place of grace's most profound moment. It is the place where my sins were atoned for by the death of Christ, the only Son of God.

And the cross was flanked by two gracious meals, the evening before when Jesus suppered with his followers and a few mornings later when Jesus made himself known over breakfast, cooking some fish for his disciples. In that post-resurrection scene, Jesus revealed himself to the startled disciples by saying, "Come and have breakfast" (John 21:12). The hospitable one served a meal to the ones who would carry his name to their deaths.

After Jesus ascended and the Holy Spirit descended like tongues of fire, the disciples of the first-century church gathered together, and the book of Acts says, "Every day they continued to meet together in the temple courts. They broke bread in their homes and ate together with glad and sincere hearts" (2:46). With the growing diversity of the church around the world, meals become the place where we minister to each other out of our weakness and in humility. We find our strength not in our unanimity on issues but in our unity in Christ.

Grace served over a meal is an essential part of how we do life together. Food is the fuel of kindness, and through a meal we break down the cultural differences that have long divided us. Hospitality calls us to bring to our table those who culturally may not be getting an invitation. The Gospel writer Luke captures this point when he records the story Jesus told about an invitation to a great banquet. The problem was, no one RSVP'd. So the second invitation was sent with instructions, "Go out to the roads and country lanes and compel them to come in, so that my house will be full" (Luke 14:23). This is outrageous hospitality.

When we open our tables—simple or elegant—to those unlike us, we are creating an image of the day when we will forever feast, as John envisions in his revelation, when he sees "an angel standing in the sun, who cried in a loud voice . . . , 'Come, gather together for the great supper of God'" (Revelation 19:17). If it's true, and I believe it is from the picture John paints, that heaven will have a great banquet; and if it's true that the epic supper is for the redeemed; and if the redeemed are people from every tribe and tongue and nation, then the only conclusion I can come to is that *that* supper table will be one colorful and multiethnic spread.

What if our tables today began to look like heaven's table then? Kindness is inviting "the other" to our tables.

When God gave Abraham the big covenant in Genesis 12, he said,

Go from your country, your people and your father's household to the land I will show you. I will make you into a great nation, and I will bless you; I will make your name great, and you will be a blessing.

I will bless those who bless you, and whoever curses you I will curse; and all peoples on earth will be blessed through you. (verses 1-3)

After God said all that he would do in the covenant, he laid out one expectation to Abraham and his descendants. They were called to be a blessing to the nations, to all people for all generations. The covenant was that through us, God's obedient people, would flow his blessing to the rest of the world, from generation to generation.

It was at a supper table where Jesus, the messianic fulfillment of that Abrahamic covenant, said to his disciples, "This cup is the *new covenant* in my blood" (Luke 22:20, emphasis added). At the table over a meal, Jesus not only talked about his death for the sins of the world, but he also talked about his life as the new covenant. The expectations remain that through his followers all nations and all generations will be blessed.

One of the ways we bless the nations is when our dinner tables include those outside of our families, those who may not dress like us or look like us or worship like us or believe like us or sound like us. That meal could be with a colleague who came from across the ocean. It could be with a widow who came from across the street. It could be with a family who came from across the tracks.

Paula and I try to find occasions to welcome people to our supper table whose narratives are far different from ours. A Kenyan family. Indonesian students. Missionary kids. International students at Thanksgiving. The easy invitation is to invite like-minded and culturally similar families to comfort us with the familiar, those with the same norms and neighborhoods and income brackets and schools. The kinder invitation, we are learning, is to supper with those who reflect the diversity of "every tribe and tongue and nation." Meals like this point to the Great Supper God will one day host.

At the heart of kindness is hospitality. Hospitality so often looks like the breadth of God's people sitting around the same table, listening to each other's stories. We might as well rehearse in the here and now for what will be a great and global banquet in the by-and-by.

One of the most overlooked passages of the Old Testament book of Nehemiah exemplifies, profoundly, this idea about indiscriminate hospitality in the midst of difficult times. The story is tucked discreetly in chapter 5.

After the Exile, the people of Jerusalem wanted to be proud of their hometown again. They began to work on the gates and doors and walls, rebuilding the city brought to rubble over the years under enemy control. But the reconstruction work took its toll. Despair was heard in the voices of the builders. They were without food because of the payless work, and all of this was compounded by a famine. These were hard economic times. The haves capitalized on the have-nots, exacting high interest rates. Greedy merchants inflated the price of grain. People mortgaged their fields, vineyards, and homes to feed their families, yet property taxes still had to be paid. Some destitute families had to sell their kids into temporary slavery to pay off greedy lenders.

For Nehemiah's day, it was the Great Depression. So what did Nehemiah do about all of this despair?

He spread a feast. He made every day a Thanksgiving meal. Nehemiah, a layman who was the contractor for the wall and was now the governor of Jerusalem, set a table for the hungry. And as chapter 5 winds to a close, the story is profoundly kind.

Here was Nehemiah the governor. And at his table eating supper with him were all kinds of folks. There were people from the city. There were commoners and nobles. He even invited those from other nations to come to his table, to enjoy the finest of Israel's fare, a glimpse of "every tongue and tribe and nation."

And Nehemiah didn't have to do this. Governors were entitled. But entitlement is the curse of kindness.

Nehemiah had every right as governor to eat alone, or with just a few of the more powerful men of the city. But he didn't. Nehemiah's banquet table was spread not for the few but for the many. And each day the governor's cooks prepared the food by taking an ox and six sheep, some hens and chickens, and they presented these wonderful dishes to the hundreds of people who came to eat. And every ten days abundant amounts of the finest of wines would be delivered in barrels to the palace of Jerusalem.

It was an ancient forerunner of *Babette's Feast*.

The invitation went out for hundreds to come and eat, to put their feet under the governor's table. The wall wasn't done. Times were hard. People were struggling to make ends meet, tightening their belts. But in the midst of these difficult days with long hours of working and little discretionary money, a supper table was set for them. For twelve years, Nehemiah said, "Neither I nor my brothers ate the food allotted to the governor" (Nehemiah 5:14).

Though the food was set aside for the privileged, he never took advantage of it. And this wasn't a one-time meal for dinner guests. His table was open every day for twelve years.

The Hebrew word is *hesed*, a word that captures lovingkindness so much that it can only be described—and inadequately—as out-of-the-box, relentless, unconditional, self-effacing, gushingly generous, God-graced, others-exalting kindness. As the Spirit of God's love shows up in our spirit of kindness, what Paul said of God's love, others will say of our kindness:

> May those who know us feel and understand, as all
> God's children should, how long, how wide, how
> deep, and how high our kindness really is. And may
> they experience this kindness for themselves, though
> it is so great that they will never see the end of it or
> fully know or understand it. And so at last they will
> be filled up with God himself. (Ephesians 3:18-19,
> paraphrase)

This is the kindness God's talking about. Kindness goes far wider and far deeper than we can ever imagine.

Maybe when Nehemiah died and entered the presence

of God, in the new Jerusalem, God gave him the nod by recalling not the wall building but the meal servings. I have to believe that what God remembers is not necessarily what we think he might.

The trowels had been set down in Jerusalem, and the mortar was drying each of those evenings. The bills were piling up for the regular wall-building people like us. And in my father's old King James Version Bible it says that "the bondage was heavy upon this people" (Nehemiah 5:18). And there was a kind leader with a heart for God who gave hope through a meal to these people on the way to who knows where.

Kindness in the form of a meal.

How have we slowed our busyness to give people whose stories are different from ours—sometimes *much* different— a chance to savor a meal with us? How have we interrupted the routine of our days to mirror this attribute of God, his loving-kindness, this God who prepares a table for us in the presence of our enemies?

A meal created from our grandmother's recipe or grilled on the hibachi is a demonstration of kindness to people who are alone or who are on their way to who knows where. The meal is such a common biblical image that it beckons us to think of our table literally as a table of redemption, where healing occurs for the downcast, where joy is shared in Christ, and where the gospel is modeled to the unbeliever.

As more and more followers of Jesus make their kitchens or dining rooms or back patios places where the table is a table of grace, we are following the example of Jesus. Eating with people is an activity we see Jesus doing frequently, with the sinners and the saints. This is where conversations take place, vulnerability in sharing a meal with those who may not be the first we think about when we want to invite someone over for supper.

I want to be among the busy people of God who decelerate enough to be kind in spirit, with an invitation to sit at our tables, to eat our food, and to be an encouragement while passing the salt. In a world that is increasingly skeptical of Christians and stereotyping from a distance, we have to restore our approach to the Jesus way, calling us to a more winsome, savvy, and mouthwatering articulation of the gospel. The path to being heard by those who do not know Christ sometimes begins over an authentic dinner conversation.

May the literal tables of our homes—as humble as they and the food on them may be—point others toward the love of Christ and that final Great Supper table under which all of the redeemed will place their feet.

Chapter 11

THE LITTLE LEAGUE GAME GONE WRONG: THE WAY OF KINDNESS IS SOMETIMES REJECTED

*If you love those who love you, what credit is that
to you? Even sinners love those who love them.*

—LUKE 6:32

One warning to those of us willing to live more radically the way of kindness: our kindness may be rebuffed, or it may even incite others' hatred and scorn. The life of kindness is not living to be accepted. It's living to be obedient. The way of kindness is self-exposing and hazardous. It compels me to open up to people I would otherwise avoid because of their different beliefs or social norms.

If we are kind simply to receive kindness back, then our kindness will wither when it gets the stiff arm or even the fist. If our kindness goes in just one direction and does not expect to be returned, then our kindness won't recoil at rejection. Then we are obeying Christ, who called us to be receivable and never promised us we'd be received.

Living to be received and living to be receivable are quite different. Kindness is living to be receivable, opening ourselves to others whether they receive us or not. Living to be *received* focuses on how others respond to us. This is beyond our control. Living to be *receivable* focuses on how we unmask ourselves in new and sometimes uncomfortable ways for others to receive us. Maybe they will or maybe they won't. Kindness that doesn't expect appreciation or a quid pro quo is the more noble way of kindness. The apostle Paul uses odor imagery to get this point across when he says we are the "aroma of Christ" (2 Corinthians 2:15). To some we'll be the smell of life and to others the smell of death. We cannot control how people perceive our Jesus scent. But we do need to give off his fragrance.

Even if our aroma of kindness is repulsive to others, perhaps someday they will notice it was Jesus they were smelling all along and experience life through him. We may be long out of the picture, and we may never know. The English Puritan George Swinnock wrote, "An empty perfume bottle still smells when the perfume is gone."[1]

I don't like to be rejected when my intent is to be received. Kindness does not always get a thank-you. It often elicits no words of gratitude. Sometimes it does the opposite of what we intend. But even if our Jesus aroma does not give off the smell of life, Jesus still calls us to the way of authentic kindness—selfless, humble, vulnerable, open, and faithful.

On a New Year's Eve in Times Square not long after college, I extended my celebrating hand to a stranger. He

extended his middle finger to me. Kind gestures are sometimes spurned.

"Love your enemies, do good to them, and lend to them
without expecting to get anything back," Jesus told a large crowd
one day who came to hear him. "Then your reward will be
great, and you will be children of the Most High, *because he
is kind to the ungrateful and wicked*" (Luke 6:35, emphasis
added). I like to be kind to the grateful. Christ calls us to be
kind to the ungrateful, to be kind in such a way that we don't
expect to get anything back. This is the audacity of kindness.

I recall from one evening long ago the subtle and unforeseen feeling of rejection, of kindness snubbed.

As a graduate student in Boston in my late twenties, I
needed a job to help pay the rent for the apartment I shared
with a schoolteacher and a first-year psychiatry resident.
Around the corner from the Brookline neighborhood where
the three of us lived stood a low-income high-rise for families
who could not afford to buy their own place or pay the going
rent rate in this pricey city. The local housing authority tried
to keep the place clean, painting over graffiti and replacing
broken windows. With all its Band-Aids, it still looked like
"the projects," the places suburbanites like me typecast as
ghetto. I frequently drove by but never stopped in.

One day, I saw a posting that the city was hiring tutors to
assist disadvantaged public school children. I applied, inter-
viewed, got hired, and showed up for my first day. My job
site was the low-income high-rise.

I pulled my Subaru wagon into a parking spot, weeds

growing recklessly between the asphalt cracks, and I sat tight for a few minutes, not knowing what I was about to begin. The sign on the first-floor function hall read "Homework Help Room." Minutes earlier, the students had descended in the lone Otis elevator with their backpacks and their questions. By the time I walked into the building, they were sitting at tables waiting for tutors like me to do what no one at their homes either could or would.

The roomful of elementary school students were African American and Hispanic. A handful of them were white kids. For the most part, life for these children in the cinder block apartments was a daily grind. Single-parent households eked out a living with no margin. Many of these kids were latchkey children, coming home from school alone before their moms or grandmothers got off work. If any adult was at home, the interest or ability wasn't there when the fourth or fifth graders needed help with spelling or math or social studies.

I made it through the first night and then the second. I finished a week, and then two. Before long, week after week, with three or four other tutors, I was easily floating from table to table, dutifully—and most nights joyfully—helping kids with their homework. When they aced tests or quizzes, we'd exchange high fives.

Kory came to the Homework Help Room every day. He was eleven and had a kind heart, once I got through his aloof veneer. He lived many floors up with his mother and siblings. To the best of my knowledge, no father posed for any of their family photos.

I'd quiz Kory on his geography, thinking how truly foreign to him places like France or Indonesia were, and even the Rocky Mountains or the Mississippi River. Kory's geography was his neighborhood, occasionally stretching to Boston's subway or bus routes.

After gradually wading into his personal life over the months of tutoring at the high-rise, I began to sense he was warming to me. He talked about his mother, who worked every day. He liked some of his school subjects; others not so much. He wanted to know about my girlfriend and me. More than anything, Kory told me about his Little League baseball team and how much he loved to play. There I sat, listening to someone's son who loved baseball, never anticipating that years later I'd take my own son across the country stopping at ballparks, seeing America from coast to coast. No dad was driving Kory to any major-league parks or eating at local restaurants across the USA.

No dad drove him to the Little League park across town.

I spent weeks of building trust with Kory, asking him question after question. Finally he took the risk to invite me into his world outside of the Homework Help Room.

"Would you come to watch me play baseball sometime?" Kory asked, explaining that his mother, who worked odd hours, hardly made any of his games.

When I told him I'd be there, he didn't give me a hug or a fist bump or flash some glistening smile, but I did sense he was glad someone would come to be his advocate, his cheerleader. Someone would be at his game to yell his name when he stepped into the batter's box or threw the runner out at first. Someone who cared would make sure his baseball games wouldn't become his unwitnessed moments. When the game was over, he wanted to be with someone who could recount his plays and affirm him as a gifted boy, encouraging him over an ice-cream cone.

Paula and I showed up at the city ballpark. We brought a blanket and sandwiches and sat by the first-base dugout to cheer our hearts out for Kory.

As the players arrived, I yelled something like "Hey, Kory! Good luck!" I wanted him to know I was there. My single intent was to be his fan. I would cheer him up if he struck out or cheer him on if he scored. My focus was to home in on one player: the eleven-year-old African American kid wearing his baseball pants and pounding his fist into his glove as he warmed up for the game.

He half smiled when he looked my way, acknowledging me in an upward nod as if a string had jerked his head backward. Kory and his teammates began throwing baseballs back and forth and taking swings with aluminum Louisville Sluggers at phantom pitches.

It was time for the game to start, but it kept not starting. Players continued playing catch as coaches from both teams huddled by the chain-link dugout. More time passed, and still no "play ball" call from the umpire. In fact, as I looked around, there was still no umpire. One of Kory's coaches came over to Paula and me, not knowing which team we preferred or which player we knew.

"Do you know how to call balls and strikes?" he asked me. "Huh?"

"The umpire didn't show up," he went on, "and we can't have a game without an ump. Do you think you might be able to officiate our game?"

"I've umped a few softball games," I answered the man asking me to change roles from advocate to judge.

"Thank you," he replied. "We really need you out there. Here's what you do. Stand behind the pitcher's mound, not home plate, and you have to make all the calls. Strike zone is knees to numbers, and we play seven innings. The rest of the rules are fairly basic if you know baseball."

Taking the coach's word that no ump meant no game, I reluctantly agreed. I *say* reluctantly, but I did sense a spike of self-importance with my newly assigned position to adjudicate on this playing field of ten- and eleven-year-old boys. If I was going to be an ump, if these coaches and players and families trusted me with the integrity of this game, then I'd be a leader—impartial, imposing, powerful, and absolute in my decisions. That's what umpires do.

I looked at Paula with a bit of pride in being the one selected, albeit from a deficient pool. She shook her head as I got up from the blanket and headed to the field, abandoning my date for the next hour to respond to the civic call of duty to be the big Little League magistrate.

Moments later, I stood behind the five-foot-one hurler starting on the mound for the team opposing Kory's.

It crossed my mind that *Kory* was why we came. I didn't

come to be his umpire. I came to be his supporter. My role had unexpectedly changed.

I can't recall the plays that led to the last inning, but that's when I stopped enjoying the role as the judge and wished I had stayed on the blanket as the boyfriend and the fan. Kory's team was ahead by a run, and the opposing team was at bat in the bottom of the seventh with a few men on base, the term *men* used loosely.

All I remember is that the batter hit the ball to the outfield, the fielder dropped it, and the at-bat team scored two runs to take the lead and win the game. Because of the ensuing cacophony of hollers, everything got muddled.

At first I thought the noise was hype for the runners rounding the bases, waved on by their coaches and cheered on by their teammates and parents. But then I realized the yelling was also coming from Kory's dugout, housing the team that had just *lost*. The screams were not for the runner. They were at the ump.

They were yelling at *me*. "He threw the bat! The batter threw the bat! He should be called out! The runs don't count!"

By now the other team was involved in the protest, yelling back that the kid didn't throw the bat.

I was looking back and forth to both dugouts while the ballpark awaited my call. There was no more order in the dusty diamond where I presided. My seven-inning reign was crumbling as my ability to rule had come into question.

It seemed like hours passed as the spectators and teams shouted their interpretation of the event. I heard a disharmonized chorus of sopranos from the Little Leaguers and baritones from their coaches and fathers. They all were awaiting my call and telling me what it should be. I had to make a decision. Whatever decision I made, one of the teams would lose. The judge needed to give a verdict.

Any popularity I enjoyed as the officiating justice of a rather uneventful game was now history.

Yelling and gesticulating people on both sides of the base paths stared and awaited my call. I looked at Paula for help from the blanket, or at least sympathy. I got neither. She was reading a book, oblivious.

I *did* know that if the batter throws the bat, he's out. But the problem was I didn't *see* it. Being the only ump, I was watching the outfielder dropping the ball, not the batter tossing the bat. Latching onto some phrase I'd heard about but never really heard, I said to the unruly crowd, "I call 'em like I see 'em, and if I don't see 'em, I can't call 'em. I never saw the bat thrown. Batter's safe. Runs score. Game's over."

I allowed the runs, not willing to compromise my fairness by the hearsay of the people under my charge those few innings. It was official. Kory's team lost.

The backlash was more than I expected. These dozen or so halfway-to-manhood boys on Kory's team displayed no respect for my judgment, muttering invectives under their breath and disrespecting my leadership.

I hadn't asked for any of this.

I looked to the dugout, and the coach who had begged me to bail them out an hour earlier was shaking his head, muttering under his breath complaints about my competence. I overheard an adult from somewhere in the crowd say something to the effect of "Hey, ump! You stink!" (Thankfully, it wasn't Paula's voice.)

The entire evening became an unfortunate rebuff of my goodwill. My act of kindness was derailed. Protests of disapproval from one dugout and cheers of victory from the other left me standing alone in this clamor of yells.

Not soon enough, the teams packed their equipment and the field emptied. I stood alone behind the pitcher's mound, wanting to be the last to exit. No one thanked me. No honorarium. No invitations to ump again. No good-byes. Even Kory left without saying a word to the only two fans who came simply to see him play that summer evening.

We didn't go out for ice cream to replay the game's highlights and for Paula and me to affirm Kory's baseball skills. Paula and I headed for the car. All the happiness that had accompanied me to the game was nowhere to be found, and I felt unappreciated. My kindness went unrewarded.

Thankfully, it was a short-lived misery. A few days later, I was back to working with Kory on his math, giving him *attaboys* and watching him smile when he got the answers right.

Kindness rebuffed is still kindness. We are not less kind if our kindness is not received. Kindness has far more to do with how we give than how others respond. If I'm kind only for the gestures of appreciation, then kindness is more about my own need for affirmation than it is selflessly imparting the virtue itself. Kindness is one-way goodness, and sometimes kindness receives no thank-you or acknowledgment or returned favor.

The way of kindness is a way of life. Over time, pressing into kindness can become a habit of the heart. It leads us to understand the difference between the *episode* of loving our neighbor and the *lifestyle* of loving our neighbor.

But venturing into the way of kindness is hard. It's countercultural. It's an adventure. It's risky. It's unsafe. Though the life of kindness is good, it's not always protected. Kindness is sometimes unwelcomed and awkward. It's admitting our own messiness and imperfections on the journey in order to invite others in. Sometimes that invitation is ignored. Sometimes it's declined. In its authenticity, kindness chances rejection. And it's a tough challenge for the more cautious or proud among us—like me—to live the way of risky kindness. The kind life is the vulnerable life, the life without charades.

If we fear rejection because it's an affront to our pride, our kindness will be timid. If we are honest in who we are and can persevere through the rejections that might come, we are living a higher dimension of kindness. Matthew 10:40, the verse my father quoted to me about making ourselves receivable, is not about being received. The point of being kind to friends and to foes is not to be respected, received, or befriended. The point is to be respectful, receivable, and friendly so that our testimony about the love of God will have its best possible reception.

I learned a word in a philosophy class back in college that I've not heard since then. The word is *eudaemonism*. I don't know why I still remember it, but when the good professor explained it, I think he was defining a part of my own depravity.

Eudaemonism is the act of doing something virtuous in order for those who notice to think more highly of you. I suppose this is also called feigned generosity or the humble brag. If generosity is the selflessness of making ourselves receivable, then eudaemonism is the selfishness of wanting to be received.

When I stop doing the kind thing because I don't feel appreciated or it's not making me feel more important, I'm not really doing the kind thing at all. Sometimes our kindness is noticed by the grateful. Sometimes it's not acknowledged at all. And sometimes kindness gets the snub.

Jesus talked about the one-way dimension of kindness when he gave the Sermon on the Mount. When you love your friends and show them kindness, it is quite easy and costs little. But Jesus says we need to love our enemies, even those who persecute us.

As Jesus sent out the seventy-two disciples, he cautioned them that sometimes they'd enter towns where they wouldn't be received. Sometimes the good news the disciples were eager to tell and the amazing work they were empowered to do was rejected. Jesus even anticipated this, and he prepared them for rejection. Luke recalls Christ's words of solidarity with his disciples whose love is not accepted, saying, "Whoever rejects you rejects me, and whoever rejects me rejects the one who sent me" (Luke 10:16, NRSV).

Rejection. We need to get used to it and get over it. Cold water may be thrown on our acts of kindness. But kindness is not about how we are received. It's about how we make ourselves receivable.

Chapter 12

MY PATRON SAINT OF KINDNESS: THE WAY OF KINDNESS IS OFTEN AWKWARD BUT ALWAYS RIGHT

Love your enemies, do good to them, and lend to them
without expecting to get anything back.

—LUKE 6:35

The way of kindness comes with risks. The way of kindness is vulnerable and unsafe. The way of kindness should not expect a thank-you and may even receive a rebuke. Living this way means taking initiative and sometimes stepping into a pile of rejection. The way of kindness is others-centered and not me-centered, which is the hardest place of all for many of us. And as my father demonstrated time after time in front of me as a witnessing boy, the way of kindness is always selfless and often awkward.

I was a child, so the particulars are lost to time. What hasn't been lost is what he did. The gall.

The office furniture store in Worcester, Massachusetts, was

room after room of swivel chairs and metal desks and stackable bookcases. My father, a frugal man of Scottish descent, scanned the room for signs that said "Sale" or "Seconds" or "Clearance." He was no stranger to these showrooms, and he was no stranger to Reuben. Reuben, a Jewish furniture merchant, ran the place. Over the years he and my father had forged an in-store friendship. As far as Reuben was concerned, my father had the friendliness mojo.

I had no idea what triggered my father to do what he did next. I know now, but it has taken decades to understand the profound beauty in what was then the mortifyingly awkward.

In one motion, my father reached out his hands toward Reuben's face, forming his fingers like prongs around a precious diamond. "Reuben," my father said to this man, the furniture salesman, "I love you." No lie.

How dare he? I wanted to crawl under the nearest discounted desk and hide.

Hugh Corey was my father, the good pastor. He has been dead for a while now. I spent my life studying him, learning from his love, standing in his shadow, and sitting at his feet. And occasionally I slunk down in my seat, humiliated. Among all the people I've known, he is the one who best taught me what it means to walk the way of kindness, living out what Jesus said to his disciples, "Whoever receives you receives me, and whoever receives me receives him who sent me" (Matthew 10:40, ESV).

Through the thirty-six years our lives overlapped, my father often quoted John the Baptist, reminding me, "A person can receive only what is given them from heaven" (John 3:27). When he received grace from heaven, my father was determined that each day others would receive grace through him. He was a conduit. The love of Christ inhabited him, an ordinary person, an ordinary parson. And he gave that love away. From him I learned that being "receivable" meant he received from God and lived that others would receive as well. He took the risk of living the way of kindness even when it was ridiculously awkward. And with him, it usually was.

He had a lot of practice engaging with the troubled and dispossessed. In some ways it was criteria number one on his job description as a small-church pastor.

Every Sunday night, without exception, he bade the troubled to the front of the sanctuary, where a long wooden altar stretched parallel to the first pew. No kneelers cushioned the legs of the souls who stooped at the rail, just space for those with woes to lay their burdens down. The Presbyterians and Episcopalians down the street lined their altars with prayer books and chalices. We, as Pentecostals, lined our altars with Kleenex boxes.

I remember sad people coming forward at my father's beckoning to kneel at the altar for "the anointing." Each Sunday night I'd join my father as he laid his hands on these humbled parishioners and prayed Jesus over them. They were longshoremen and seamstresses, unemployed and aged. There were lonely men and mothers with children born "out of wedlock"—those words said in hushed tones to keep things on the level of prayer and not gossip.

As they knelt by the dozens at the altar, I would follow my father as he prayed with fervency and volume over each bowed head. He heard their intercessions. I heard them speaking in strange tongues. He looked at their prayer-contorted, tear-moistened faces. God looked at their souls. I looked at their bent legs, careful to step around their calves as I followed him from sinner to sinner, each in God's eyes a saint.

The menu of their requests was long. People wanted prayer for healing, filling, saving, refilling, delivering, reconciling, comforting, sustaining, sanctifying, providing, and protecting. He patiently prayed over every head bowed. This was one of the most profound ways I, the curious child, watched him demonstrate kindness.

Whenever my father prayed, he prayed out loud. As a boy I would stand outside his study at home with my ear cupped against the door. I listened to him pray for me, for us, for the world, and to receive the Holy Spirit's "unction," a word he liked to say. A small man with a deep voice who prayed with great earnest, he would cry out to his Lord on his knees, saying over and over, "Master, master, master" while I listened outside. I felt comfort in his voice, knowing the pureness of what he did behind a closed door. As a boy I didn't yet know that what happened behind preachers' closed doors was not always as honorable.

And when my father emerged from his study, he exuded the love of Christ. His spirit of radical kindness to his family, to his colleagues, to his neighbors, and to strangers was forged on the anvil of prayer. He didn't pray to be kinder.

He prayed to be more like Jesus. Kindness seemed to follow that prayer. Profound and unconditional kindness was a by-product of his passionate pursuit of Christlikeness. It was the fruit of the Spirit.

The kindness fruit showed up not just in our home but also around almost everyone he met. I recall few encounters with shopkeepers or waitresses when he didn't ask questions or offer encouragement, when he didn't make himself receivable. Usually, he was unashamedly kind.

Those moments were often awkward—at least they were for me, his shy and self-conscious son. He hugged the local Sunoco station attendants who pumped gas into our family's Pontiac Bonneville, because he truly liked them. The name patches sewn on their shirts read Mohsin or Faheem or Mohammed. As he hugged, I slouched, lower and lower in the sedan's backseat, wanting him to let go and move on.

The afternoon my father dropped off his sole-worn shoes, he asked the Armenian cobbler—whose name sounded like Kardashian—to pray with him over the polish-stained counter. He reached out, and their hands linked until the prayer was over. I kept an eye on the doorway, hoping no one would come in and catch them in the act of talking to God.

I was embarrassed then, but more recently I'm embarrassed by that childish embarrassment. Those days I thought my father didn't know when to keep to himself, didn't know when just to shake hands. But now I see him more accurately: a humble man who went out of his way to demonstrate kindness to so many he encountered—not just those he knew or agreed with.

His modus operandi was simple. He believed Jesus died for the Middle Eastern man changing his oil *and* for the elderly couple living in the house next door who probably checked "none" on religious affiliation surveys. As far as my father was concerned, kindness called him to love them, too.

He made himself receivable, though he was not always received. His friendly smiles, kind words, and waves to strangers were occasionally met with a brush-off, a scowl, or even a finger.

Pride more than anything else gets in the way of kindness, and it shows up in our aversion to being scorned. If we extend kindness in order to be received and thanked, we will dole out kindness only in safe places, places where we know we'll be accepted. But when our kindness has to be anonymous, when our kindness is met with ingratitude, when our kindness gets the stiff-arm, then we often get offended. This is pride, not kindness. Kindness delivered is sometimes awkward and sometimes rejected, but this does not make it any less virtuous. The more we press into kindness in situations when we know it may not be received, the more selfless and Christian that kindness is.

Someone recently told me we never lead our enemies toward following Christ, only our friends. Kindness is how we try to make our enemies our friends, even if they refuse to accept our overtures. If we're always thinking it's us against them, we won't get very far. We can't influence people who are our combatants. The power of kindness can do what the power of caustic arguments or arm-twisting can never do. If I don't take this kindness idea seriously, especially among those with whom I disagree deeply, then how will they ever see in me the profound, reconciling, unmerited, and sin-forgiving love of Christ? Too often we make the issue about who is right.

I recall the words from J. D. Salinger's *The Catcher in the Rye*: "The mark of the immature man is that he wants to die nobly for a cause, while the mark of the mature man is that he wants to live humbly for one."[1] We're called to live the humble way of kindness. By Salinger's account, for what it's worth, then we're the mature ones.

These moments of my father's generous kindness and my own awkward reticence were elemental memories during my elementary years, early in the 1970s, while we were still living in church-owned housing. With each of my father's unin-vited embraces and unrequested prayers, I'd blush, although I suspect that, subconsciously, I was also tucking away a lesson on how Christ calls me to live the radical way of kindness when it doesn't come easily.

My father also showed me that having a kind spirit is not the same as having a pliable core. He would strike up a con-versation on Saturday with a plumber whose language was as dirty as his job, and on Sunday—behind the pulpit—he spoke in biblical tones of strength and resolve and certainty and calling. I saw no gap between how he treated others and what he said in his sermons. He lived with a firm center and

soft edges, following Jesus' affirmation of greatest command-
ments (Mark 12:30-31). "Love the Lord your God with all
your heart and with all your soul and with all your mind and
with all your strength." This was his life of a firm center. And
"love your neighbor as yourself." This was his life of the soft
edges, the receivable life, the outrageous way of kindness.

I think about him today as I live in a culture increasingly skeptical of Christians and one that stereotypes them
from a distance. I have learned from my father that living the
Jesus way calls me as it called him to the winsomeness of the
gospel. The path to being heard by those who do not know
Christ sometimes begins through our lives of kindness, as
risky and awkward as this may be.

My father's kindness was sometimes received, but it
was often rebuffed. In his naiveté he usually didn't see the
snubbing coming, and when it happened, he continued
undaunted. When new neighbors moved in across the street,
I watched from our front window as my father guilelessly
brought them a welcoming gift of Vermont maple syrup. A
few minutes later he returned, jug in hand. "They don't want
it," he told me, putting it back in the kitchen cabinet. That
day, and at many moments like it, I felt for him the rejection
that he never seemed to feel for himself.

My father got the kind thing in a deeper way, understanding Christ's call to be kind to ingrates, even—and
especially—when it was awkward.

Chapter 13

THE KINDNESS EXPERIMENT:
SEVEN THOUGHTS ON SOFTENING OUR EDGES

*Be kind and compassionate to one another, forgiving
each other, just as in Christ God forgave you.*
—EPHESIANS 4:32

Soon into my time on the team at Biola University, a pastor stopped me after another one of my rookie-year speaking engagements and said one sentence as he walked out the door: "If I could give you some advice as you start this job, spend more time on what you are for than what you are against."

"I will," I said, a bit unsure of what he meant. His admonition kept replaying in my mind over the next few weeks. "Spend more time on what you are for than what you are against." I kept thinking of the many things we need to be against, those sins that need to be overcome in ways that lead to reconciliation and justice. We must be against racism, human trafficking, pornography, rampant materialism, inflated pride, bad theology, and the list goes on.

But I didn't think that's what he meant. I tracked down his name, and I wrote to ask him why he had said that to me.

He responded in a thoughtful letter with gentle words of counsel for me, still on the front end of leading a university with thousands of students who follow Jesus. He unpacked his words by saying that those outside the church will never be won over by watching evangelicals clad in razor wire lobbing accusations at each other *or* at the secular culture. He believed it's a new day for a winsome Christian witness without a diluted gospel message.

The kind life, the receivable life, errs on the side of what we're for rather than what we're against.

That sounded a lot like my father's words to me when I was a ponytailed, twentysomething researcher trying to figure things out. I flashed back to the talk on being receivable, a conversation he providentially passed on to me in 1991 while we walked the dirty streets of Bangladesh's capital city. While living in what missiologists call the 10/40 window, I encountered Matthew 10:40: "Whoever receives you receives me, and whoever receives me receives him who sent me" (ESV). While living amid overwhelming crowds of people who knew little about Jesus, I learned about making myself more receivable.

When my patron saint of kindness told me about the receivable life, it was like Elijah's mantle draped over me, the understudy Elisha. And like Elisha, I'm hoping for more of what my mentor had, not less. Elijah said to Elisha when he was about to cross the river, "Tell me, what can I do for you before I am taken from you?" and Elisha replied, "Let me inherit a double portion of your spirit" (2 Kings 2:9). I want a double portion of the Jesus spirit of kindness my father had. It's what I pray for, and even though I continue to fall woefully short, I'm still going for it.

Since that mantle moment, I've found myself asking that inward question: *How do I live a life that is* more *receivable,* more *radically kind?* Lately, I have been asking that question about not just what it means to be a receivable disciple, but also what it means to be a receivable church, a receivable nongovernment organization, a receivable for-profit company, a receivable university. What would happen if we as leaders resolved that the convictions of our organizations stayed firm while our edges riskily and radically softened?

I remember when I arrived at Biola University, I began giving stump speeches about how each of our students has the potential to change the world. I don't say that anymore. It's not because I don't think they will be influential. It's because I don't think it's the goal. Nobody single-handedly has the capacity to change the world. Christians tend to love extra-large strategies that pledge to impact the world in short order. We've tried this time and again, and we've accomplished very little. We need to take the long view through respectful collaborations and earnest conversations, all done in the spirit of kindness.

I've eased up on the hyperbolic language about how each

of us has the potential to be a world changer. Life in Christ is less about our results and more about our character. This was Jesus' point. Make yourself receivable. Don't be fixated on outcomes. Let's not get hung up on the ambition of being *received* when Christ has simply asked us to be *receivable*. Living this way can be more profoundly transforming than the political posturing or the power plays that have defined many Christian strategies for many years.

As we live receivable lives with firm centers and soft edges, we begin to cast an aroma that is the aroma of Christ. As more and more of us live this way, that collective aroma will waft widely, and we will be known as a people committed more to what we are for than to what we are against. We are for reconciliation. We are for excellence in the arts. We are for unburdening the marginalized and oppressed. We are for life's sacredness. We are for sound business ethics. We are for safe communities. We are for healthy relationships and marriages. We are for, above all, the atoning and renewing work of Christ.

Jesus said that those who receive us will receive him and will receive his Father who sent him. Our task is to live the daily, faithful, at times awkward, self-deflecting way of kindness. We do this as Christ-redeemed disciples. And we do this as Christ-centered communities, smelling like Jesus.

The aroma of Christians is a mixed bag today. Some are giving off the fragrance of Christ, and others are giving off no fragrance at all, or actually smell like something other than Jesus and the God of the Scriptures.

If as Jesus' followers we took much more seriously the spiritual discipline of living fragrantly, we'd open the pathway for those who receive us to receive Christ. What if more and more followers of Christ made a covenant to live lives lavishly kind? If this generation began to say, "I'm choosing the way of kindness," it's possible a renaissance of civility would begin through us.

Maybe for a while we need to turn down the volume, listen more, and err on the side of head-turning kindness, which is not necessarily what our culture is expecting from us. Maybe as Christian leaders—skilled in our professions and grounded in biblical wisdom—we need to recalibrate our agendas toward service rather than power. Those of us who lead this way, from a posture of kindness and not callousness, will have a greater influence than ever before. Those who continue the path of belittling or backstabbing or battling will be marginalized from the most important conversations, or they'll simply sing to their own choirs. Let's keep beating our swords into plowshares.

It was Adoniram Judson Gordon, the nineteenth-century Boston pastor and half the namesake of Gordon-Conwell Theological Seminary, my former vocational stomping ground, who said, "Our task is not to bring all the world to Christ, our task is unquestionably to bring Christ to all the world."[1] A lot has changed on the landscape since A. J. Gordon penned those words in the 1800s, but it's our task nonetheless.

Bringing all the world to Christ sounds like domination. Bringing Christ to all the world sounds like kindness.

Kindness calls us off the soapbox and into the cities and villages where we live the life of grace. How can the way of kindness empower us to be less inward looking—bringing all the world to Christ—and more externally winsome— bringing Christ to all the world? And how do we do this without forsaking our most cherished beliefs? As our culture seems to be accelerating in a direction that is not consistent with our Christian values, we have some options.

We can respond to the pressures of our day and choose to lead our organizations toward a more "not of the world" posture. This is the way of isolationism, of circling the wagons and in essence being sidelined. Or we can respond to the pressures of our day and choose to lead our organizations toward a more "in the world" posture. This is the way of conformity, of rolling over and compromising our convictions to fit in. Or, rather than a middle ground between the two, we can find a higher ground as we become organizations, churches, and companies committed fully to both truth and grace, the first of these virtues defining our centers and the second defining our edges.

Markus Bockmuehl, who teaches at Keble College at the University of Oxford, talks about institutional humility as an *ex-centric* orientation. By ex-centric he means we take our focus outside our walls and think of ourselves in the service of the wider world and public good. It's the "do justice" and "love kindness" and "walk humbly" of Micah 6:8.

This is what poet Richard Wilbur had in mind when he said, "Love calls us to the things of this world."[2]

How do we do this as leaders? How can the church continue as a vibrant and winsome witness in the world, needed now more than ever before? Below are seven thoughts I've pondered on how we might position ourselves away from *isolation* on the one side and *conformity* on the other. The higher ground, not the middle ground, is to consider new and enhanced ways to extend our organizations' reach with humility, with confidence, with influence, and yet without capitulating on our deeply held and time-honored convictions. It's the Christian story of living as resident aliens.

1. A firm center and soft edges means we become more involved in the culturally unfamiliar.

If we're engaged with those who are unlike us, and others see our organizations as places where we reach outward for good things to happen, it's going to be a lot harder for us to be criticized or even penalized for what some believe are out-of-date principles.

Having a spirit of kindness positions us much better to silence hostile voices. Not all hostile voices, but many of them. When we are in the cultural crosshairs, and these moments will come more and more, I want leaders in our cities and in the public square to say, "That's the church that works with the city helping undocumented children. That's the Christian college partnering with HIV research or helping to draft a policy for urban educational reform. That company is hiring special-needs employees or setting up a foundation to beautify the neighborhood. That's the campus ministry hosting conversations with voices of differing perspectives." Absent these collaborations, we could be defined merely as anti-this or anti-that organizations rather than as organizations that stand *for* something.

But if this is all we're about and we lose the heart of Christ's message that he came to save sinners, then we've lost our firm center in our efforts to soften our edges. We need both.

And we need both because of the pressure we'll increasingly face to isolate ourselves or to give up our convictions. In what some call our increasingly post-Christian culture, a rapidly growing sense of misunderstanding if not suspicion is leveled at organizations with biblically grounded values. Christians are becoming a religious minority and a sexual minority in that our sexual ethics are seen as obsolete. So if our default is *only* to protect our tribe by identifying *only* with organizations like us, we will be increasingly peripheral to meaningful cultural conversations. We need to think about those groups of people who might say, "Christian organizations would never link with us," and see if perhaps we can.

Those who identify as evangelicals also need to understand they have common bonds on some core values with many Mormons and Catholics, Jews and Orthodox Christians. So why do we keep such a wide gap between us? Horizontal relationships sometimes do a lot to minimize the vertical differences, even if our biblical values seem to others inconsistent or even bizarre. This is leaning into kindness by building better bridges. The days of competition and going it alone need to end. Not only is collaboration and partnering on areas of common values the way the rising generation chooses to get things done, it's also the biblical way to get things done.

I am convinced Christians have much to contribute to mainstream academic societies, to professional associations, to public policy, and to media commentary. Brilliant Christians have worked hard and studied deeply to "be prepared to give an answer to everyone who asks [them] to give the reason for the hope that [they] have. But do this with gentleness and respect" (1 Peter 3:15). The first part of this verse is the firm center. The second part is the soft edges.

We need to be at the leading table of conversations in philosophy, science, technology, entertainment, the arts, media, urban planning, commerce, and education. We need to be grappling with the big issues of the day, not as soloists or as an evangelical tribe, but with those whose worldviews are radically different from ours. We should not be reluctant to collaborate with others whose faith might not fit ours, to look for opportunities to join together in ways that lead to the common good, those areas we agree are right and just. My friend and Gordon College president Michael Lindsay puts it this way: "Just because we don't see eye to eye does not mean we can't work shoulder to shoulder."

As we do this, others who may not agree with our positions may back down on their stereotypes that Christians' ideas don't matter. This is one of the ways we live out our kindness in an increasingly post-Christian culture.

We may need to think of ourselves more like Daniel, as

exiles in Babylon, than like David, as citizens in Jerusalem. We need to dismantle our inferiority complex and our mimicking tendencies by creating and articulating ideas that are innovative, and we need not retreat to conferences and conversations where all the voices sound like ours. That's intramural sports, and we need to stretch beyond our safe circles.

Our influence as leading Christians will increase for the good and for the cause of Christ if in the mainstream sectors of society we are seen as leaders and not followers, innovators and not copiers, conversing from the center and not hollering from the edges. We need to be risky collaborators and not go it alone. This is the way that makes us more receivable.

A healthy Christian organization understands the balance of stretching our thinking while respecting our biblical framework. We must be intentional in inviting other voices into dialogue and to present their ideas in a way that is conversational and respectful.

I encourage us to think about this carefully. We need to dialogue with those of other faiths or no faith at all, because if we do this right, we'll model for our communities how to dignify those who believe otherwise and how to have an intelligent conversation respectfully. Who knows where this might lead in our own understanding or in someone seeing Christ in us?

I've been trying to do this over the past year by engaging with presidents of local Southern California universities to simply share a meal and a conversation. If I were not intentional about stretching into these conversations, I believe my silence would reinforce stereotypes about the institution I lead that are basically untrue. One of the prayers we don't pray enough is the prayer for favor, what Jesus experienced as he grew in favor with others (see Luke 2:52). That prayer for favor has been on my lips more and more, not for our sake but for radiating the grace of God.

Living the way of kindness means opening our doors to others so they see our graciousness and experience our hospitality. When leaders model this, those we lead will learn how they might also be gracious and caring without being either weak willed or in your face.

How we do this will take some thought, but we should not be afraid of contrasting ideas, nor should we close our doors to those who are willing to come for a respectful conversation. If we are not opening our homes for others to come, and if we are not accepting offers when others open theirs, we will be increasingly isolated without much opportunity to be the aroma of Christ. Few notice soft edges from a distance.

2. A firm center and soft edges means we are creators of goodness and beauty.

Christians need to keep pressing into beauty and goodness. My ongoing desire is for Christians to create more beautiful things through music and the visual and media arts, as writers and performers and storytellers and movie producers. And let's extend our creative work beyond the bordering streets of our organizations. If God is the author of all things beautiful, we become his fragrance as we fan the flames of imagination and invest in the many arts: written, culinary, spoken, visual, dance, digital, and on we go. This is the way of kindness.

Sadly, Christians were once at the table for conversations on the arts but have over the centuries lost their prominence. This is being recovered as a generation of Christians are recapturing artistic expressions of the imagination rather than mimicking the artistic expressions of others.

I am convinced we have more and more to contribute to the arts. Just think of what would happen if we extended beauty and goodness beyond our own organizational walls. Just think what would happen if we reached across the gallery to collaborate with artists with radically different frames of reference. What if suburban parochial schools rented a city theater for a play or leased space in the arts district for a gallery? What if a suburban church and an urban church combined their choirs so that the performers truly looked and sounded like Revelation 7's gathering of every tongue and tribe and nation? We can be communities that attract artists and intrigue those who love beauty regardless of their perspective on faith. When we do this, we are making our edges soft without tampering with our centers. The way of kindness means we generously explore beauty and goodness. It also means we don't quickly cast scorn on art that disturbs us, instead reflecting critically and generously on distortions of goodness and beauty.

I thought about this as I read a letter sent to an art professor at the university where I serve:

> Dear Professor Anderson,
>
> I just finished viewing your ARTS 315 lectures on YouTube. I would like to commend you on the course, which I found interesting, erudite, and intellectually stimulating. I recently received a PhD in Film Studies . . . so I was interested in learning more about avant-garde visual art.
>
> As an atheist, I must confess that I was a bit hesitant to view lectures from Biola University. I suppose that I half-expected to be subjected to the rantings of some preachy, benighted, Bible-thumping philistine. I was very pleased to find your course subverting such stereotypes through its rigor and sophistication. . . .
>
> I am very thankful to have encountered your exemplary lectures—in addition to greatly enhancing my knowledge and appreciation of contemporary art, they have helped make me a better instructor. Thank you.

As I've interacted with Professor Anderson since that letter came, he shared his view that the letter writer's reference to "preachy, benighted, Bible-thumping philistines" was perhaps a reference to those "Christian commentators who impatiently foreclose on modern and contemporary art because they don't know what to do with artists who eschew beauty and goodness as the primary aims of artmaking." And sadly, he added, in the bigger academic art world, the most common labels attributed to such Christians are ignorance and unkindness, both of which can be detected in the letter writer's tone.

In the art world today, kindness is more than creating beauty. It is a generous spirit of listening to artists whose worldviews are incongruous with our own. And kindness also means considering their work with dignity and intellectual honesty. When we do this, we move the conversation forward.

3. **A firm center and soft edges means we approach the growing opposition in our day by leading with humility.**

Something's changing in our culture. And I say this not as a fighter or a right-winger. I was never a member of the Moral Majority. I don't always see eye to eye with friends who belong to the NRA or who have harsh views on immigration. And I'm not prone to buying into conspiracy theories. So when I say something's changing, I'm saying this from a measured perspective. What has happened in the last few years is staggering.

There has been a shift in the way Christianity is seen by those outside the church, despite the fact that the percentage of churchgoers has not changed over the past fifty years. To the progressives in the United States who pride themselves on tolerance, Christians are increasingly intolerable. The depiction of Christians in our culture is often made up of caricatures and misinformation more than it is of truth.

Part of the antagonism is the work of the enemy. And we are standing for biblical virtues that many in our culture basically cannot stand.

But a part of the reason why Christians are increasingly less tolerated is that our conversations are in-house, and we're not making connections to the wider world as intentionally as we could.

We need new and more conversations that build bridges and not walls. I applaud my friend Gabe Lyons and his brilliant Q Ideas forums to help us embody the gospel and be restorative voices in culture, working toward the common good and doing so in conversation with those who may not believe as we do. We need these conversations more than ever. It's easier to be kind when we are in the dominant position, but this position is no longer ours. To be heard, we need to have civil voices and thoughtful ideas. This will take more work from our minority position. The Jewish community, a religious minority like we may be becoming, has long seen the academy and culture-shaping institutions as places where they should invest their time and talent, with no little influence.

Not long ago I was in my office talking about convicted civility with University of Chicago church historian Martin Marty, who wrote in one of his books, "People today who are civil often don't have very strong convictions. And people who have strong convictions are not often very civil."[3] I commented to him how we need universities that embody both conviction and civility: firm center, soft edges.

We must continue to be among the relevant voices by creating conversations and reaching outward, engaging in the marketplace of ideas with a gentle and respectful voice that will be heard. The risks are too high to do otherwise. We don't need to be part of the arsenal. We need to be part of the dialogue.

When we act this way, we will be less on the defensive and more in a position to be heard and understood, though not necessarily agreed with. And though at times we need to fight to hold our ground, the benefits of opening ourselves to civil conversations outweigh the risks of shutting out other voices or of solo saber rattling.

4. A firm center and soft edges means we fear not when our grace is met with hostility.

I've said earlier in this book, but it's worth repeating, that being received and being receivable are quite different. Living to be *received* focuses on how others respond to us. This is narcissism, and it's beyond our control. Living to be *receivable* focuses on how we open ourselves in new and sometimes uncomfortable ways for others to receive us, whether they choose to or not. This is kindness, and it's within our control.

When the apostle Paul writes to the church in Corinth about how we need to be the *aroma* of Christ, he says that some will sense our aroma as the "smell of death" (2 Corinthians 2:16, NLT). We are seeing this around the world today as more Christians are being persecuted and killed than ever before. Jesus never said we would be received. He actually said that often we'll be rejected. When Jesus sent out the Twelve, he gave them authority to drive out evil spirits and to heal sickness and disease. As he sent them, he gave them a caution because he knew there would be many wolves dead set on destroying them. "I am sending you out like sheep among wolves," Jesus warned his closest followers. "Therefore be as shrewd as snakes and as innocent as doves" (Matthew 10:16).

Kindness means loving our enemies in a gentle, dove-like way. Kindness, however, is not naive. Living the way of kindness means we accept that we'll be rejected. But we must also be aware that there are not only those who will ignore us but also those whose intent is to crush us. Discernment and wisdom are components of kindness.

Kindness means we won't back down on speaking out against the Satan-smelling evil in the world. Hatred, racism, violence, exploitation, and greed all smell like the devil. We need to be concerned about and combat the spirit of this age that is rampant. We need to stay strong in our faith and fear not, despite those who are committed to upending the message of the gospel and who refuse to engage in gracious conversations. We need to be aware of the growing nihilism in our society, the rejection of principles based on moral reasoning and biblical truths, leading to a belief that life is meaningless. We need to strengthen our resolve against the truthless and graceless claims of radical religious types globally who would rather choose violence than collaborate toward peace. We need to face these movements as the people of God with steadfastness through the power of the Holy Spirit.

As disciples of Jesus, we are not called to be nice. We are called to be kind. Niceness lacks convictions. Kindness has a soul, and it has fire. Kindness doesn't cave in, but it calls us to stand strong and to communicate intelligently, theologically, and irenically to counter those on both sides who are talking politically, heatedly, and thoughtlessly. Leaders who don't pander to culture but open themselves to new and creative ways of speaking into culture, as uncomfortable and as messy as it may be, will find the risks worth it.

Through the ages, God has honored his remnant who willed not to bend their godly convictions in order to be accepted. "But they did what was right in the eyes of the LORD" is a popular Old Testament refrain, describing the kings who chose not to capitulate when the cultures around them tried to woo them away. Other kings "did whatever was right in their own eyes." We are called to be the former kind of leaders.

In many ways, Christians today are in the middle of a centrifugal force pulling us away from our centers. To survive, leaders are wondering where to draw the line between firm centers softening and firm centers staying true.

Roberta Ahmanson, a public intellectual, philanthropist, and dear friend, wrote a letter exhorting me to stay the course and not to trim our university's sails to prevailing winds. That letter was so meaningful to me, I had it laminated. She wrote:

I remind us both of Augustine. 410. Rome (*Rome!*) is sacked. The world has ended or is about to.

People are fleeing the heartland, some wind up in
Hippo at least for a while. Augustine sees. We are
dual citizens. The City of Man. The City of God.
We have loyalties to both. Jesus made that clear.
But our first and final loyalty is to the City of God.
The Israelites often forgot that; it's *so* easy to do,
surrounded by the prosperity of the Canaanites and
the beauty of their gods. But Augustine knew the
truth and he wrote it. We are there again, Barry,
and we all have to choose. City of Man? City of
God? Our brothers and sisters in the past have
faced the same choice. Until Jesus comes, who
knows how many times we will have to face it? We
are in one such time right now. And, you are close
to the eye of this storm. Be not afraid.

5. **A firm center and soft edges means we remain even more
   deeply rooted in biblical faithfulness.**

For us to have firm centers, we cannot let down our commitment to the authority of Scripture. A lot of this book may
sound to readers like I'm more interested in soft edges than
firm centers, and some might say that's exactly what's wrong
with the church. Wasn't it the mainline, soft-edged Protestant
church of the late 1800s that abandoned the authority of
Scripture and the salvation by grace alone through faith
alone, leading toward the emergence of the social gospel?

Much has been written by many thoughtful theologians
calling us to biblical fidelity. I encourage readers of this book

to spend even more time with good biblical commentaries, to delve into the study of Scripture, and to think biblically about all of life. We need both firm centers and soft edges to truly live the receivable life Christ calls us to.

I'm overcompensating in this book for grace, the virtue that has sometimes been eclipsed in our conversations by truth. The need, however, is for both. I had the honor of attending the memorial service of the Christian leader Charles Colson, who has been quoted as saying, "Without *truth*, grace can be deceptive. And without *grace*, truth can be debilitating." The people of God must strive to be communities that will forgo neither grace nor truth. Jesus himself, the Word who "became flesh and dwelt among us," was "full of grace and truth" (John 1:14). Not half of each, but full of both.

Recently I was in a small gathering of Christian leaders in San Francisco, and one of the participants, a leading pastor named Dan Kimball from Santa Cruz, wrote me a few days later. He was chagrined that too many churches and universities have gone soft on teaching theology and have "focused more on justice/compassion to the almost exclusion of doctrine/apologetics." He went on to say,

> I think 10–15 years ago (pre-Bono) the evangelical
> church was too heady and not enough justice.
> But now we have had two or three generations of
> teenagers going through high school who do not
> have doctrine, apologetics, etc., and it is more about

justice/compassion which . . . I think . . . can wear
off—as why do you need to be a follower of Jesus to
help the poor? Atheists help the poor. Buddhists help
the poor.

Dan's right. The knowledge and relevance of the Bible is
in decline in our society *and* in our churches. But the good
news is many Christians are not part of that trend. We need a
growing remnant that cares deeply about fidelity to Scripture
and is doing something about it. Being kind is not just about
grace. It's also about truth.

The reason why we live the way of kindness—the reason
why we need to be a Matthew 10:40 receivable people—is
not so that the world will be a better place, à la John Lennon.
The reason is that we believe the grace of God needs to be
seen in us so that those who do not know Christ will experience his saving grace and the forgiveness of sins he offers.

6. A firm center and soft edges means that evangelism is at the heart of why we live this way.

In the past century, we as Christians have been known for
our evangelistic tradition, our commitment to the gospel.
In recent years, however, there's also been a growing renaissance of the compassion and intellectual tradition alongside
our evangelistic tradition. The time-honored calling of the
church to start hospitals and rescue missions and schools
has been overtaken by others of no faith at all. My hope
and prayer is that we move forward in both of these areas

again—the gospel in spoken proclamation and through tangible acts of mercy—and I see it happening.

I have been talking about this with other college presidents who are likewise concerned that the zeal for evangelism as a biblical mandate could be replaced by good works to assist the physically suffering and broken. Our compassion emphases as Christians are many and essential, but we must do this as a means and not an end. We care about human suffering because we care about eternal life.

Paul makes this connection clear in Romans 2, asking the people of God, "Do you . . . not [realize] that God's kindness is intended to lead you to repentance?" (verse 4). The kindness of God is the grace of God, something we do not deserve, nor can we earn it. Absent a *true* commitment to the *true* gospel, we risk going the way of many before us who misapplied this verse and lived as if it said, "Don't you realize that God's kindness is intended to lead you to your own acts of kindness?" But kindness points people to the Cross and not to us. The Cross was the kindest moment in history, when God demonstrated how great is his grace. Sins forgiven. Life made new.

When you think about kindness this way, it is truly an image of the transformational grace of God, who loved the world so much that he gave his only Son for us. As we live kindness, we bear witness for Christ in a fallen world, and what an impact we are making as we do. Kindness leads to repentance. It is evangelism in its essence. Kindness is not merely good works to improve someone's life. It leads to new life in Christ.

"Be kind and compassionate to one another," Paul writes to followers of Jesus. How does he say we do this? Paul says compassionate kindness is "forgiving each other, just as in Christ God forgave you" (Ephesians 4:32). Kindness looks like forgiveness—forgiving each other in a way that points to how God forgives us.

What's encouraging is that many churches and organizations, colleges and social service agencies have not jettisoned evangelism for mercy ministry. It's not a choice between the two, but it's the gospel at work in both. The life of kindness is the life of loving our neighbors *and* our enemies. We live the way of kindness because Christ died for them, so the least we can do is to love our Muslim neighbor and our Jewish colleague and our agnostic nephew.

In a world increasingly skeptical of Christians and stereotyping from a distance, we have to restore our approach to the Jesus way, calling us to a more winsome and savvy articulation of the gospel in word and in deed.

7. **A firm center and soft edges means we need to remember that Christ-centeredness means we will never be marginalized.**

The marginalization of Christian organizations is an idea I have been reflecting on recently, and this has spawned some of my thoughts about how we can lean into the way of kindness. Some Christians fear that if we become marginalized to our culture, we will lose our influence.

I have intentionally avoided the word *marginalize* in describing the place of the church. The reason I've tried to avoid that word is because I do not believe Christians are becoming a marginalized people or our institutions marginalized organizations, nor should we harbor this fear. I say this because marginalization has everything to do with our perspective of the center. If we define the center as the mainstream of the scholarly academy, we will be marginalized. If we define the center as American cultural and political trends, we will be marginalized. If we define the center as being among the top one hundred trendsetting churches, we will be marginalized. If we define the center even as historic Western evangelicalism, we will be marginalized. These are not our centers.

Christ is.

Only three times in the New Testament is the word *center* used, and each reference is found in the book of Revelation describing the position of the Lamb's throne. John the Revelator says, "The Lamb at the center of the throne will be their shepherd; 'he will lead them to springs of living water'" (Revelation 7:17). We know that in the end, the resurrected Christ—the Lamb of God—will rule and reign. So perhaps as we stay the course as Christians have done through the ages, committed to the truth of God's Word, the centrality of Christ's atoning work, the presence and power of the Holy Spirit, and grace lived out in the way of kindness, we will be the ones abiding at the center.

May our Christ-centeredness endure and remind us that we are not, nor may we ever be, a marginalized people. May we be careful to align around the constant Center, true through the ages. This is what I mean by a firm center.

May we not take for granted that we can and should stand apart among so many churches and organizations today. We stand apart because we have not let go of the centrality of Christ and the authority of Scripture. Firm centers. We stand apart because the heart of our organization has never lost the heart of the gospel of grace. Soft edges.

As we move forward as the people of God, I also pray that we move in the love of Christ and the power of the Spirit so we all understand that the same Spirit that raised Christ from the dead dwells in us.

Firm center, soft edges. A spirit of kindness does not mean a pliable core.

"Whoever receives you receives me," Jesus said, "and whoever receives me receives him who sent me." We live this way as our highest calling. Firm centers and soft edges will be our greatest mark of living the way of kindness. May this generation of Jesus followers be known as a generation that is epic in life because we are epic in love.

I would like to think that our best days are still to come in being an influential voice in the world. The secret to being this way is neither new nor novel. It is for us to be clear on our ideological core but not triumphalist in our spirit.

And with a firm center, we can explore the edges with more confidence and humility.

Leadership with a firm center and soft edges is Christlike leadership, far more about carrying a staff than a scepter. It's the Moses example far more than the Pharaoh example. When God beckoned Moses from the burning bush and called that backcountry shepherd to a radical career change from tending sheep to leading his people out of Egypt, Moses responded by bending down and unstrapping his laces, standing barefoot in the presence of God.

My prayer is that Christian leaders, churches, organizations, universities, and on and on will be communities of barefoot followers of Jesus. May we understand that leadership and servanthood are about unlacing our shoes when God calls us, not wearing army boots to stomp on our brothers and sisters or to kick Christianity into the public square. As I noted earlier, barefoot is the position Jesus' disciples took as he washed their feet, teaching them about being servants and telling them to go and do likewise.

My prayer as a university president is that the rising generation of Christians engages the culture with a deep conviction in truth, but in a way that is meek, loving, and gracious. I care far less whether they have tattoos inked on them or this or that pierced. What I care about is that they live biblically with a firm center and soft edges. No fist shaking. No saber rattling. We need to be people who give off the aroma of Christ, the smell Paul describes to the early Christians living in a pagan culture.

We do this better by understanding Jesus' call to be receivable in Matthew 10:40. It's often the verses preceding

10:40 that get the attention, important words of Christ to his disciples about following him and carrying the cross. But then Jesus says, "Whoever receives you receives me, and whoever receives me receives him who sent me." Being receivable keeps our edges soft. Revealing the one who will be received keeps our centers firm.

And they'll know we are Christians by our love.

CONVICTION, COURAGE, AND CIVILITY

If you remain in me and my words remain in you,
ask whatever you wish, and it will be done for you.

—JOHN 15:7

Kindness looks a lot like respectful conversations and charity.[1] Incivility looks a lot like fragmentation and polarization. When you pan the political and cultural landscape today— seen through the lens of news outlets and partisan politics— it looks like incivility is winning. But if we call that winning, it doesn't seem like much progress is being made. It makes me wonder if the problem isn't incivility's imbecility.

About the time this book was written, Biola University's Center for Christian Thought hosted a conference called Disagree. Christian thinkers from far and wide gathered to ponder how we engage with others in areas where our disagreements are sharp but our words aren't.

Gregg Ten Elshof, the Center's director and professor of philosophy, wrote about why Biola would have a conversation like this, saying,

> Disagreement is an inescapable fact of life. We can't outrun, outsmart, or out-love it. It's here to stay. And, if we learn how to interact with it well, it can be a powerful resource for learning, for love, and even for growth into deep and abiding unity. But usually it's not. Usually it divides us, angers us, and brings to the surface our deepest fears and insecurities.[2]

This conversation is the message of firm centers and soft edges, when we, in the words of the conversation planners, "pry disagreement away from the vices which so often accompany it and to harness its power for good."[3] As Christians, we need this modeled for us like never before, given the vitriol and the fragmentation that seems to be increasing rather than decreasing. How do we winsomely engage in conversations in the context of disagreeing on worldviews, social issues, politics, race, economics, war, immigration, gun control, and even the gospel itself, even the existence of God? We need modelers who show how we can flourish in the context of disagreement.

This takes Christians who embody courage, conviction, and civility. Ideological hard-liners don't need to be idiotically hard shelled. Diplomacy between archrivals sometimes requires a relational dynamic that builds trust without bending principles. As followers of Jesus, we need these three virtues. Conviction without courage goes nowhere. Courage without conviction goes anywhere. Conviction with courage goes somewhere. When civility unites conviction and courage, the force toward reaching that "somewhere" is so much greater and points toward the lordship of Christ and the Kingdom of God. Christians who are in leadership roles will be wise to take seriously the virtues of conviction and courage and then clothe them in a winsome, kindhearted spirit. Only then do I believe we'll make progress on the seemingly intractable challenges of our day, challenges that are paralyzing us.

Conviction is the virtue that binds us to our most cherished and least changing beliefs. It grounds us in the truth and forms our theological core. Courage is the virtue that calls us to bold action, reaching beyond the horizons of possibility. As Christians we are called to be a present witness within our culture. We do this by melding conviction with courage, guided by civility that bears witness to the gospel.

In the twentieth century, evangelicals and fundamentalists differed on matters of strategy and goals when it came to bearing witness to the gospel within our culture. Do we roll up our sleeves and engage our culture as redemptive voices, as many from a more Reformed perspective have argued? Or are our efforts merely tantamount to rearranging the deck chairs on the *Titanic*? Jesus' coming is imminent, so our main concern should be winning the lost and not involving ourselves in cultural redemption. Do we give up, or do we take over?

This was the question many Christians were asking in the 1940s and 1950s. Their answer was engagement rather than disengagement. They believed the walls of separation among Christian groups would begin to come down and the effect of their gospel witness would go up when they worked together.

Today, as president of a Christian university, I believe this same partnership approach is the way forward. We need a generation of Christians with deep convictions regarding what is true, grounded in Scripture. We need a generation of Christians courageous in their faith, empowered by the Holy Spirit. And we need a generation of Christians whose demeanor is civil, kind, and compassionate. The days of going it alone or fostering a spirit of competition need to give way to fresh partnerships and collaborations that stretch beyond our theological and denominational differences.

We have come a long way as followers of Jesus in this past century. Christians are in positions of public leadership at the highest levels and are influencers of the arts. They are prominent urban leaders and are running major corporations. And they are unapologetic about their faith. The church is being renewed as God raises leaders committed to his Word, who welcome the empowering work of the Holy Spirit and who are winsome in their witness. Christians continue to emerge as thought leaders and as scholars, winning the widest academic respectability. And the gospel is raging like wildfire in the Global South, where the epicenter of Christianity is now moving.

At the same time, hostility toward the Christian world-view is not abating, in the United States or abroad. In fact, a secularization of culture that tacks toward post-Christianity—what some would call nihilism—is under way in the West. And persecution of the church globally, despite waves of renewal, has never been more rampant. Our task is to redouble our efforts to be people of conviction, courage, and civility, virtues our world needs to see in us, and through them to see the gospel. With deep-seated convictions from a biblical foundation, we must approach the brokenness of the world without defensiveness, aloofness, or anger. To be responsible citizens and leaders to the communities God has called us to, we must be winsome and bold, neither elitist nor combative, known more for what we are for than for what we are against.

We must engage our culture with a deep conviction in truth, but in a way that is meek, loving, gracious, and fragrant. We engage the culture with temperate tones by serving alongside and not casting stones from pedestals.

For centuries, followers of Christ have been addressing the world's brokenness with divine love by acting compassionately, creating beauty through the arts, championing the great Christian intellectual tradition, and proclaiming the gospel in word and deed. This witness erodes when Christians take it upon themselves to respond with anger and acidic spirits. Equally condemnable as those who are angry are those who are aloof.

When conviction and courage are guided by civility,

Christianity has the potential to look a lot different ten or twenty years down the road. It very well may be bereft of political partisanship and no longer societally defined by cultural wars. Or we may be like aliens in a culture increasingly hostile to followers of Christ. If that is true, may we press forward with conviction, courage, and civility even more.

How we respond to the shifting of tectonic plates now under way may well test the church as it has throughout the ages. These testing times have been Christians' finest hour. With a world that is more accessible through technology, with a nation that is more ethnically diverse, with the interreligious dialogue more at our doorstep than ever, with some of the faith's historic values under siege, Christians are being closely watched. Cultural complexities and global connectedness are part of our daily lives.

Amid these changes, the truth of Scripture even more must fortify our deepest convictions, fuel our courage, and call us to lives of gentleness. This means exercising the virtue of kindness and exorcising the spirit of condescension. May we demonstrate the love of Jesus Christ by our faithful obedience to biblical conviction, by the strength of our Spirit-breathed courage with the tone of Christian civility.

May this generation of Jesus-followers be characterized by their courageous faith and by their humility and grace. May their simple civility and their kindhearted goodness cover their zeal as they stand for Christ, come what may.

GRATITUDE

I owe a lot of thanks to a lot of people who helped me get this book written. My soulmate, Paula, and our three children—Anders, Ella, and Sam—loved me through my writing with patience and insights and, of course, kindness. My gratitude for them gets first dibs.

Friends and family—like my octogenarian mother, Esther, who prays for me every day, and my sister, Bonnie—kept me going. To the brothers who know me inside and out, thank you for your encouragement on the journey, including this leg of writing. Among others are Dan Munkittrick, Meirwyn Walters, Doug Green, John Truschel, George Deligiannides, John Orfinidis, Jerry Fiske, Larry Acosta, Jay Luthro, Mike Erre, and Don Headlee. I'm indebted to my mentors, Dr. Robert E. Cooley and Dr. Walter C. Kaiser Jr., who poured into me when I had little to pour back.

The community and board of trustees at Biola University have been exceedingly kind in their encouragement. I'm especially grateful for the current and past Biola board chairs,

Wayne Lowell and Stan Jantz. Wayne has been wise and gracious every time I needed counsel. Stan is a writer and cultural exegete. His recommendations, support, and frequent words of wisdom kept me focused and motivated amid all the other spinning plates. I work each day with an amazing team of university leaders, a team I love and find it a joy to count as colleagues. These women and men are motivated and extraordinarily gifted, and I count it an honor to work with them year in and year out. I have the privilege of serving alongside a remarkable faculty at Biola who take their calling as teachers, scholars, and mentors with utmost seriousness. And each day I come onto campus, I'm reminded of the loyal and skilled employees—followers of Jesus who keep the university strong and moving forward. Brian Shook and Michele Hughes not only administer the president's office with aplomb, but they are my consciences for time stewardship. The space they have provided and protected made this book possible.

To my peers in other Christian colleges and universities who are likewise striving to do the presidential thing with firm centers and soft edges, I am honored to be in the crucible of leadership shoulder to shoulder with you.

Biola students, so much of this kindness stuff reminds me of you and is for you. You breathe life into my job, every day. Live kindly.

A few others in Biola and beyond warrant special attention. A number of writers and thinkers gave me good counsel on many of the book's chapters. Paula has been my wisest editor and most candid counsel, loving me with her perceptions. For edits and perspectives, I'm also indebted to Brett McCracken, Paul Buchanan, Aaron Kleist, Bill Robinson, Tim Muelhoff, Gregg Ten Elshof, Tamra Malone, Beck and Julie Taylor, and David Horner. Longtime friends Dick and Ruth Foth opened their home for me to write and think and eat and write some more. Peggy Campbell did the same. Phil Cooke motivated me to start writing the book. Thanks to my agent, Greg Johnson, who guided me through the publishing process, and to the good folks at Tyndale, who have demonstrated patience and perspective throughout my final stages of writing. Among them are Jonathan Schindler, Jon Farrar, and Ron Beers.

So many have shown me kindness. May the good virtue live long.

NOTES

CHAPTER 2—A NEW JOB, A ROAD TRIP, A FATHER AND SON:
THE WAY OF KINDNESS IS MESSY
1. Eudora Welty, *One Writer's Beginnings* (Cambridge, MA: Harvard University Press, 1984), 44.
2. H. L. Mencken, *Prejudices: Second Series* (New York: Alfred A. Knopf, 1920), 158.

CHAPTER 3—THE SECURITY OFFICER ON DAY ONE: THE WAY OF KINDNESS LOOKS LIKE HUMILITY
1. Marilynne Robinson, *Gilead* (New York: Picador, 2004), 30.

CHAPTER 4—THE GAY CONVERSATION IN DHAKA: THE WAY OF KINDNESS WHEN WE DISAGREE
1. Laurie Goodstein, "Evangelicals Open Door to Debate on Gay Rights," *New York Times*, June 8, 2015, http://www.nytimes.com/2015/06/09/us/some-evangelicals-take-new-look-at-bibles-stance-on-gays.html.
2. Barack Obama, "Remarks by the President on the Supreme Court Decision on Marriage Equality" (briefing, The White House Rose Garden, Washington, DC, June 26, 2015), The White House: Office of the Press Secretary, https://www.whitehouse.gov/the-press-office/2015/06/26/remarks-president-supreme-court-decision-marriage-equality.

CHAPTER 5—UNSUITABLY INTOLERANT: THE WAY OF KINDNESS OFTEN TAKES TIME
1. John Inazu, "Pluralism Doesn't Mean Relativism," *Christianity Today*, April 6, 2015, http://www.christianitytoday.com/ct/2015/april-web-only/pluralism-doesnt-mean-relativism.html.
2. Wesley Hill, *Washed and Waiting* (Grand Rapids, MI: Zondervan, 2010), 17.

CHAPTER 9—THE FIDDLER AND THE GERMAN BOY IN WAITING ROOM A: THE WAY OF KINDNESS MENTORS

1. Anne Lamott, *Help, Thanks, Wow: The Three Essential Prayers* (New York: Penguin, 2012), 86–87.

CHAPTER 11—THE LITTLE LEAGUE GAME GONE WRONG: THE WAY OF KINDNESS IS SOMETIMES REJECTED

1. Richard Rushing, ed., *Voices from the Past* (Edinburgh: Banner of Trust, 2009), 316.

CHAPTER 12—MY PATRON SAINT OF KINDNESS: THE WAY OF KINDNESS IS OFTEN AWKWARD BUT ALWAYS RIGHT

1. J. D. Salinger, *The Catcher in the Rye* (New York: Little, Brown, 1951), 188.

CHAPTER 13—THE KINDNESS EXPERIMENT: SEVEN THOUGHTS ON SOFTENING OUR EDGES

1. "Missionary Mottoes," *All the World*, Board of Foreign Missions of the Presbyterian Church in USA, January 1909.
2. Richard Wilbur, "Love Calls Us to the Things of This World," *Collected Poems, 1943–2004* (Orlando: Harcourt, 2004).
3. Martin E. Marty, *By Way of Response* (Nashville: Abingdon, 1981), 81.

CONCLUSION—CONVICTION, COURAGE, AND CIVILITY

1. Sections of this chapter have been extracted from my chapter in *Christian Leadership Essentials: A Handbook for Managing Christian Organizations*, ed. David S. Dockery (Nashville: B&H, 2011), chapter 14, "Engaging the Culture."
2. Gregg Ten Elshof, as quoted by Quinn Clark, "Conference to Explore Charting a Course to Reconciliation and Better Public Discourse," *Biola News*, March 11, 2015, http://now.biola.edu/news/article/2015/mar/11/conference-explore-charting-course-reconciliation-/.
3. Ibid.

ABOUT THE AUTHOR

A native of Boston, **Dr. Barry H. Corey** has been president of Biola University since 2007. He previously served as vice president for education at Gordon-Conwell Theological Seminary. Corey received a BA in English and biblical studies from Evangel University and an MA in American studies and a PhD in education from Boston College. As a Fulbright scholar, he lived in Bangladesh, where he researched educational programs for children of the landless poor. He and his wife, Paula, live in Southern California and have three children: Anders, Ella, and Samuel.

MORE RESOURCES
TO HELP YOU
LOVE
KINDNESS

Explore **Open Biola** for thousands of free educational resources from Barry H. Corey and other Biola University faculty members — including biblically centered lectures, classes and articles.

OPEN.BIOLA.edu